SPIRITUAL
HEALING

SPIRITUAL HEALING

Everything you want to know

LIZ HODGKINSON

GUILD PUBLISHING
LONDON · NEW YORK · SYDNEY · TORONTO

Acknowledgements

For expert help and information, the author would particularly like to thank: Don Copland, Shirley Brooker, Matthew Manning, George Chapman, Dr Bernard Grad, Mary Russell, Ursula Fleming and Allegra Taylor.

This edition published 1990
by Guild Publishing
by arrangement with
Judy Piatkus (Publishers) Ltd, London W1

CN 5712

Printed in Great Britain

❧ Contents

❦ *Introduction*

By all the known scientific and medical laws, spiritual healing shouldn't work – but it does. Or, at least, it can.

There are far too many documented cases of seriously ill people being made well by spiritual healers for the phenomenon to be dismissed as rubbish. Even the most prejudiced sceptic cannot deny that apparent healing miracles have occurred – not just in biblical times, but in our own century, here and now.

Spiritual healers have made blind people see and deaf people hear; they have been able to straighten spines and make the lame and crippled walk. They have not yet been able to walk on water, but they have effected many cures that were unattainable through conventional medical treatment. In fact, spiritual healers usually only see patients once they have been given up by their doctors. There can never be any guarantee of a cure, of course, and reputable present-day healers certainly do not promise any miracles. But the fact that anything happens at all – ever – is in itself astonishing to those of us who have been brought up in the rational, scientific tradition.

Most modern spiritual healers are not medically trained. Many are not even educated in the formal sense. What has happened is that these apparently ordinary, everyday men and women have discovered, usually by accident, that they possess some unusual gift of healing. At some stage in their lives, they have laid their hands on somebody, or perhaps just sent out a healing thought to a person in distress, and there has been unusual benefit. Very often, nobody is more surprised than the healer when the gift is discovered.

1

Shirley Brooker is the headmistress of an infants' school in Eastcote, Middlesex. She now also works as a healer, but had no idea of her abilities until 1971. She said:

My life was very unhappy at the time, and I went to a clairvoyant to try and sort myself out. A cat I had then was extremely ill, and seemed to be about to die.

The clairvoyant told me, much to my surprise, that I had healing powers, and that if I stroked the cat's back at the same time as sending out a healing message, the cat would recover. I did what she told me, and within two days my cat was completely better. I was astonished.

From those modest beginnings Shirley has gone on to heal family, friends and many others who thought they were beyond hope. For the story of how she enabled a bright young teenager to escape from his wheelchair and lead a normal life, see p. 154.

We live in an extremely unspiritual, materialistic age, and yet spiritual healing is currently enjoying the most phenomenal growth. More and more people are becoming healers, it seems, and more and more of the seriously ill are seeking out such healers. Because of this the subject is at last being investigated scientifically. The scientists, mainly in Britain and America, who have investigated healers have had no choice but to come to the conclusion that something strange can happen in a healer's presence. Healers have, under laboratory conditions, been able to induce seeds to germinate, slow down the destruction rate of blood cells, influence the activity of animals, and alter the brainwaves and workings of the nervous system in humans – simply by laying on of hands, or by concentrating on the object and consciously trying to influence it from a distance. Non-healers have usually not been able to effect these changes, however hard they may have concentrated. Nor have doctors. In fact, in one experiment, seeds treated by medical students grew more slowly than those left to grow by themselves, without any 'treatment'.

The consensus of opinion of all the scientists who have worked with healers is that something which seems to be paranormal is happening. Healers definitely do appear to have powers that the majority of people do not possess – but the definition of exactly what those powers are has so far eluded conventional science.

All this is very hard for conventional doctors, who have spent seven long years learning about the body and all its functions, to accept. To the average doctor, the most annoying aspect of spiritual healers is that often these people don't know anything about medicine, have had no training – and yet can often apparently heal the patient when the doctor can't. For many years, conventional doctors tried to dismiss spiritual healing as nothing more than the power of suggestion. But now, increasingly, they are admitting spiritual healers into their surgeries, as they have found that these people can make a positive difference to their patients. A few doctors are even discovering a healing ability in themselves – something they perhaps ought to have anyway! And since 1977 spiritual healing has been allowed by the British Medical Association as an adjunct to orthodox medical treatment; spiritual healers are now welcomed in many NHS hospitals – not to supplant doctors and nurses, but to work alongside them.

We could say that spiritual healing has come of age. But what exactly is it? What is this mysterious ability that some people seem to have, to enable a patient to be healed without the intervention of drugs, surgery or any other healing tool – and without, in most cases, any medical knowledge? Will it help you? That is what this book attempts to find out.

Spiritual healing has a very old history. In ancient times it was generally believed that all illness was caused by some kind of sickness or disharmony within the spirit – that part of themselves which human beings could not see or feel but which nevertheless was their most important aspect. In ancient Egypt, Greece and Tibet all healing was spiritual. But as scientific medicine progressed through the centuries, spiritual healing more or less died out in the Western world and came to be regarded as superstition and nonsense. It also, unfortunately, came to be allied with the occult and witchcraft, and those who professed to be able to heal – without being recognized doctors or surgeons – were often considered to be in league with the Devil.

Modern spiritual healing has made great efforts to overcome this deeply ingrained fear and prejudice, but even nowadays vestiges remain. Many people who have had no contact with spiritual healing feel that there is something occultist and slightly 'black magic' about it! The suspicion lingers on. But it is becoming ever more respectable, and is no longer a tiny, apparently cranky movement. The National Federation of Spiritual Healers, founded in 1955 when spiritual healing was at a very low ebb in its fortunes, now runs workshops and courses all over the country for potential healers. Members of the NFSH have to abide by a strict code of conduct, and they also have their own insurance scheme, for which the premium in 1990 was 80p a year. The reason it is so low is that no one has so far ever taken out a claim against a spiritual healer.

Detractors of spiritual healing have said that there's nothing mysterious about it, that it is purely the power of suggestion, known as the placebo effect, or the charisma of the healer which brings about the healing response. Also, detractors claim, many illnesses and diseases go into spontaneous remission anyway, and it is impossible to say that this has been due to the spiritual healer's abilities.

But although the personality of the healer may account for the success of some instances of healing through physical contact, it cannot explain the effectiveness of what is known as absent healing. There are cases on record of people in Australia starting to feel better at the same moment as absent healing is being 'sent' to them from England. And it's not only humans who respond to absent healing. Animals and even plants have begun to recover when a healer sends out healing messages over a long distance.

Spiritual healers themselves are in no doubt about how they are able to operate. They say that they are channelling some kind of divine or cosmic energy which they are able to make available to those who need it. It is a gift that they have been given, they say, and they have decided to utilize it for the service of humanity.

Spiritual healers also believe very firmly that the ancients were right and that all illness, physical as well as mental, is a manifestation of some kind of disharmony or dysfunction within the soul. Healers say that they work basically at the level of the soul or spirit, rather than that of the body. They address the soul, not the body, and direct the healing energy to the non-physical aspect of humans. If the soul responds, then the body can be healed.

This century has witnessed the work of some truly remarkable healers. One of the earliest was the American Edgar Cayce, who after entering a trance could accurately diagnose illnesses and prescribe treatments for people, often at distances of hundreds of miles. Fortunately, Cayce left voluminous notes and documents about his work, and these have been minutely examined by doctors and scientists. He appears to have been completely genuine: all his life he was a devout, practising Christian, and there has never been any suggestion of fraud. How did Cayce do it? What was he doing? Science still has not discovered the answer – but we do know that he was astonishingly accurate in his medical work. In common with most spiritual healers, he had had no formal medical training.

In Britain, one of the most successful healers of the twentieth century was Harry Edwards, who did much to give modern spiritual healing credibility. At the height of his powers, in the 1950s and 1960s, Edwards was filling the Albert Hall and Trafalgar Square, where he healed very many desperately sick people simply by laying his hands gently on them.

Then there is the strange case of George Chapman, the former Aylesbury fireman who, in a state of trance, performs 'spirit operations' apparently under the guidance of Dr. William Lang, who died in 1937. Again, no fraud or trickery has ever been associated with Chapman, and his successes are well documented. The 'operations' are performed using invisible instruments on the 'etheric' body, which is supposed to be an exact spirit replica of the physical body.

One of the youngest and most successful healers of present times is Matthew Manning, born in 1955, whose apparent powers have been extensively tested by British and American scientists. The reluctant conclusion they have come to is that Manning does display paranormal abilities – or, at least, abilities for which science has no simple explanation.

There is the possibly even more amazing phenomenon of the psychic surgeons of the Philippines, who can apparently pull tumuors and teeth out of living flesh without causing pain, leaving scars or even drawing blood. Again, many of these healers have been closely studied by scientists looking for evidence of fraud and trickery. In some cases chicanery and sleight-of-hand have certainly been detected – but in by no means all instances. Some of these peasant healers do seem to be completely genuine, and to exhibit mysterious abilities.

Spiritual healing is, I believe, growing at such a phenomenal rate because ordinary medical science is simply not meeting the needs of sick people. True, there have been wonderful medical advances over the past few years – test tube babies; heart, liver and lung transplants; enormous leaps in the treatment of burns and of accident and war victims. But at best, these advances can benefit only a very small number of people; medical science has not yet found a cure or effective treatment for most of the common chronic ills that are the curse of modern society – heart disease, stress-related complaints, cancer, migraine, allergies. And it is the chronic conditions that spiritual healers mainly treat. These are the illnesses, they say, that start in the soul – that have their origin in fear, anxiety, depression or some other kind of spiritual problem.

A few years ago, like most people who considered themselves to be rational, educated and sane, I was extremely suspicious of those who set themselves up as spiritual healers. I felt I needed to be extremely wary of anybody who was claiming special powers, and tended to keep my distance from such people. To tell the truth, I was slightly afraid of them – they formed part of a world I didn't much want to confront. If I was ill, I would go to the doctor and get treated properly. I didn't want to have some weirdo laying hands on me and muttering strange chants.

Now, though, having investigated the subject of spiritual healing with as open a mind as I could muster, I no longer feel like this. Through meeting a number of healers, I have learnt that most of them are quite ordinary people – not Rasputins in disguise, not creatures from outer space, not people who want to 'take over' my consciousness or exert their influence.

Although there may be some questionable people who set up as spiritual healers, they are not in the majority. Most of the present-day ones look just like you and me: they wear ordinary clothes, drive ordinary cars, live in ordinary houses and have families, dogs and gardens – just like anybody else. They do not wear strange robes or mutter incantations over bubbling cauldrons. They are often middle-aged men and women who have worked in other professions as surveyors, secretaries, engineers (but rarely doctors) – and who have discovered a healing gift in themselves. This ability to heal has become so marked that many of these people have given up their other jobs to practise as full-time healers.

I have come to have tremendous admiration for the work that spiritual healers are trying to do. Most are genuinely motivated by a desire to help their fellow humans, and do not seek to become rich and famous through healing. In the old days spiritual healers did not charge, but now their services are in such demand that they have to, for they have no time to make a living by other means. Most, though, just charge enough to enable them to get by; indeed, genuine spiritual healers say that the healing gift tends to vanish whenever greed, lust or ego are present.

Of course, some healers are greedy and egotistical, and some abuse their powers; but I have found that they are in the minority. It is also the case that the healing gift itself varies considerably. Some healers enjoy truly remarkable powers, while others possess a much more modest gift. In this they are like painters, pianists or any other creative artist – the degree of talent differs from person to person.

All genuine spiritual healers, however, deny that they have any actual power to complete the healing process: all healing, they maintain, must ultimately be self-healing. They claim that at best they are a kind of firelighter that sets the whole thing in motion, a starting point that helps to unblock energies in the patient and sets the process going.

You will find that there are very many different types of healing. In Britain, 'spiritual healing' nowadays specifically denotes that type of healing – contact or absent – which is practised by the National Federation of Spiritual Healers. Such healers do not belong to any particular religion, but all believe we are basically and most importantly spiritual beings. Spiritual*ist* healing denotes that type of healing where a medium goes into a trance and invokes a discarnate entity to help with the healing process.

Then there is Christian Science healing, which relies on the power of prayer to bring about the healing response. Christian Scientists, unlike spiritual and spiritualist healers, do not work with doctors, and do not use the medical profession if they can possibly help it. There are also a whole host of other mini-branches of spiritual healing – colour healing, aura healing, radionics, Kirlian photography, past-life therapy, rebirthing, crystal and gem healing. One only has to go to an alternative health exhibition to discover just how many different kinds of non-drug, non-surgical healing there are around today.

Although spiritual healing has come to be seen as a branch of alternative or complementary medicine, it is not exactly the same as these. It is quite different from, for instance, homoeopathy, acupuncture, the Alexander Technique or chiropractic. These are specific therapies for which training is required, whereas a spiritual healer may operate without any training at all.

If science is so wonderful, we may ask, how is it that it hasn't managed to get to the bottom of spiritual healing? The answer is that, although it is commonly believed that spiritual healers can harness some kind of 'energy', nobody has yet been able to explain what that energy might be; it seems to work quite outside known scientific laws.

Whatever it is, it does not depend on faith. Spiritual healing is not the same as faith healing, since patients do not need to have faith in order for it to work. You can consult a spiritual healer in as sceptical a frame of mind as you like, and you still have every chance of being healed. The only requirement on the patient's part, say healers, is a sincere wish to be well. Unless that is present, the spiritual healer can do little.

The upsurge of interest in spiritual healing, and its belated acceptance by the medical profession, will no doubt prompt further scientific investigations into what it really is, and why some people and not others possess the gift. For spiritual healing has undoubtedly become a very important development in the treatment of chronic and serious mental and physical illnesses.

In the meantime, this book provides an introduction which will, it is hoped, enable you to have a clearer understanding of what it is all about, and to learn how you too may be helped by this mysterious and valuable force.

PART I

1 ❧ *What Is Healing?*

At first this question seems easy enough to answer. Healing is the business of making sick people better.

What is illness?

But in order to understand exactly what healing is and how it might work, we have to ask what is meant by illness, and what are the basic differences between being sick and being well. These are questions which have intrigued humanity since the beginning of time – and we still can't say we have the exact answer. We are still searching, after thousands of years, for the secret of permanent well-being.

We can say that illness is any dysfunction or disharmony in the body or the mind, however this is caused. When we are well we have no diseases, no invading viruses; we have plenty of energy, we do not need medication, we sleep well and wake up refreshed, we have no eating or weight problems. All our internal organs are functioning as they should, and our bodies serve us well. In addition, lack of illness means that there is no fear, anxiety, depression or chronic anger. Healthy people are those who wake up each morning feeling positive and full of energy, looking forward to each day and being able to fulfil their utmost potential, both mentally and physically, throughout the day.

If we have a cold, a cough, flu, cancer or heart disease, we can say for a certainty that we are ill, that we have a definite diagnosable medical condition. But to be ill from flu is not the same as being ill from cancer. Flu is caused by a virus entering the body, whereas cancer happens when the body's own cells start to grow in chaotic, uncontrolled and toxic ways. Flu usually clears up of its own accord, whereas cancer is a life-threatening illness which may or may not respond to medical care.

But even if we look at a usually non-serious illness like flu a little more closely, we can see that it's not just a simple matter of a virus invading the body. Why is it, when there is a flu epidemic, that some people succumb while others don't? Although we all know that the flu virus is infectious, we also know that it doesn't infect everybody who comes into contact with it.

We know now that people are more liable to succumb to flu and other viruses when their resistance is low – when their body's immune system is not protecting them the way it should. But why is some people's resistance low? Why should some immune systems be more resilient than others? Is it because of diet, lifestyle, environment – or that intangible but fashionable condition known as 'stress'?

The importance of the mind

Although all illnesses have physical manifestations, the results of a large body of research say that the mind plays a major part in the development of illnesses. The so-called Type A person – high-achieving, restless, impatient – is more likely to succumb to heart conditions, whereas the person who suppresses anger and harbours resentment is at risk of developing some kind of cancer.

But then, we have to ask, what is the mind? Is it just the brain – that highly complicated computer inside our heads? Or is there some non-material aspect which cannot be seen, measured or quantified, but which nevertheless influences everything we do? What is the nature of 'thought-power'? Where do our thoughts come from? Doctors, philosophers, scientists and scholars have asked these questions for thousands of years. We still don't know all the answers, despite the fact that over the past thirty years or so more research has been undertaken into the nature of illness than at any other time in history.

On the one hand, scientists in laboratories have been peering down microscopes to track down ever more elusive viruses and have been concocting chemicals which 'offer new hope', as the current phraseology has it, for victims of cancer, heart disease, arthritis, migraine and other conditions which continue to evade a cure. On the other hand there is the 'holistic' movement in medicine, which says that we should not treat a single part but look at the whole person – mind, body and spirit.

An unhealthy society

One reason why the holistic movement has grown up, and is getting bigger all the time, is that, in spite of having so many doctors and hospitals, so many laboratories, so many drugs available, our health is simply not improving. Although it is commonly believed that, thanks to medical advances, we are living longer than ever before, this is simply not true. Gerontologists – those who study the process of ageing – have discovered that human beings should actually live for around 120 years; but in fact the general life expectancy has not changed for millennia. The reason that we seem to be living longer is that fewer babies and children are dying – and this ups the statistics. The life expectancy for adults – around seventy-two years – has not changed for at least a hundred years, in spite of all the medical developments which have taken place in that time.

It is certainly true that very many of the infectious diseases of the past – smallpox, diphtheria, polio, cholera, typhoid – have been all but wiped out. Some diseases, such as smallpox, have been globally eradicated while other terrors of the past, such as leprosy, are lessening their hold all the time.

But as fast as terrible diseases of bygone days disappear it seems that others, just as bad, come in to take their place. The biggest one of recent years is AIDS, but there are many other diseases which weren't even known or which were extremely rare fifty or sixty years ago: candida, hyperactivity in children, allergies, myalgic encephalomyelitis (ME), cervical cancer. Then there are the mental and psychological conditions – schizophrenia, anorexia nervosa, compulsive eating, alcohol and drug abuse, depression, panic attacks, anxiety – all of which appear to be on the increase. So far medical science has been powerless to touch these.

There are also a whole range of what are now called sub-clinical conditions where the patient does not have a diagnosable illness, but is never really well. Such people may feel generally under the weather, tired, lethargic or lacking in energy for no discernible reason. At any rate, there is no shortage of customers for hospitals, doctors, private health insurance schemes, and the ever-growing number of alternative or complementary therapies – acupuncture, homeopathy, osteopathy, aromatherapy, chiropractic.

Doctors are now, at last, realizing that diet, nutrition and lifestyle play a large part in keeping well. They are advising patients to eat a high-fibre, fresh, natural diet and to try and reduce stress. There is now a huge market in the developed world for vitamins, minerals and supplements of all kinds, and we are trying to exercise more, to relax consciously, and to cut down the amount of industrial pollution with which we are poisoning the environment and ultimately ourselves.

We are trying so hard. And still we're not well. Whatever the definition of illness might be, we know we're not well because we don't feel good. Even if we haven't got an actual disease, most of us will often be aware of fear, anxiety, nausea, headaches, backache, pains here and there. Why do our bodies play us up? Why don't they behave themselves?

It's often said that much illness in the body is caused by drinking, smoking and eating the wrong sort of diet. Yet everyone knows people who do all the wrong things and seem perfectly well, while others who carefully and conscientiously eat a wholefood diet, keep regular hours and never smoke or drink are always in poor health. It seems there must be more to health and illness than seems the case at first.

Healing – the positive approach to health

The medical profession works hard at dealing with our health problems, but all too often it touches only the symptoms and fails to put its finger on the underlying cause – hence the phenomenon of the repeat prescription. The object of healing, as opposed to medical treatment, is to reverse diseased states, to help the afflicted person towards a healthy body and a healthy mind – for good. There is a big difference, for example, between healing and going to the doctor for some pills to

alleviate headaches. If we are healed, we shall be better for ever
– or, at least, for a long time; whereas if we take a pill for a
headache, we may get the pain back again a few days later and
never really understand why it keeps recurring. Healing implies
some kind of permanent and positive change, some dramatic
difference. This can only be achieved through working on the
source of the illness.

Divine retribution?

In ancient times, it was believed that illness came about through
breaking universal laws and causing disharmony. Disease was
God's revenge on you for breaking his laws. This idea has not
finally vanished – until a few years ago, a large body of opinion
seriously held that AIDS was a divine punishment meted out to
homosexuals, prostitutes and drug abusers. When it was
realized that haemophiliacs could be infected with the AIDS
virus, and babies could be born with it, that tune was changed.
But the idea that illness is a kind of judgement from on high has
never completely gone away.

In the days before psychiatry and the scientific investigation
of mental states, it was widely believed that mental illness
resulted from evil spirits entering the afflicted person's mind. In
some primitive societies this view is still held. We in the
sophisticated West affect to know better, but the truth is we still
have no real idea what causes schizophrenia, clinical depression
or chronic anxiety; we have no idea why some people get
depressed while others, with the same external circumstances,
manage to stay cheerful.

Addressing the spirit

Healers, as opposed to orthodox members of the medical
profession, reckon that their success comes because they *do*
know why people become ill. There is, they believe, something
unhealthy in the spirit when illness of any kind manifests itself
within the body. Healers believe that our bodies are like an
automobile, while our spirits, souls or essences – the non-
material aspect which they are convinced each one of us
possesses – are the drivers. Following this analogy, it doesn't
matter how perfect, new and well-serviced the car, even if it is
a Rolls-Royce, it will not perform well if the driver is asleep or

drunk, does not know how to drive or has no idea of the direction or how to read road signs. Although all cars vary, none will perform at maximum potential unless it has a competent driver.

Spiritual healers are convinced that their job is to address the spirit – and then, with any luck, the body will respond. To continue the car analogy, even the very best driver in the world won't get a wonderful performance out of a beat-up old banger with no petrol, that hasn't been serviced for years. Healers accept that the body needs looking after, and that the diet and general lifestyle should be healthy. But they believe that illness goes much deeper than simply something going wrong with the mechanisms of the body. In a very direct way, they say, our mind, spirit or essence will affect and pervade every aspect of the body. And, until people accept that they have a spirit, they can never be truly well.

Of course, very many orthodox doctors would not go along with this. In our present agnostic society there is a great reluctance to admit the possibility that human beings have souls at all. Geneticists, molecular biologists and even some theologians believe that we are simply a mass of chemicals and genetic codes, and that eventually all will be explained in physical terms.

It is difficult to prove the reality of something which doesn't seem to exist, at least in measurable terms, but healers work on the conviction that humans, and possibly animals too, must possess a soul or spirit of some kind. They believe that there is simply not enough energy in matter alone to bring about all the changes that occur in living things. Also, they say, nobody has yet convincingly explained personality, emotions, habits and talents in terms of chemistry, hormones, genetics or environmental influences.

All this talk of the 'spirit' or 'essence' throws up another question: what is the difference between a healthy spirit and an ill, or suffering, spirit? You can tell if a person has a tumour, or an enlarged heart, by examination and diagnosis; but how do you tell if somebody has a diseased spirit? For spiritual healers, that question would be easy enough to answer: if there is any kind of illness or malfunction either in the mind or body or both, then the spirit is not healthy. Consider the situation in terms of a television set. If we are getting a poor picture, this may be because the reception is bad. But we don't know that there is anything wrong with the reception until we turn the set on. In other words, it is only the manifestation of the problem which tells us that something is wrong.

The pathway to healing energy

Healing, as opposed to going to the doctor or hospital where we will receive treatment for a specific complaint, works on the assumption that the entire universe is pulsating with beneficial energy and that we can choose to tap into this energy. A healthy spirit, or soul, is in contact with healing energy, whereas an unhealthy soul is experiencing some blockage that bars the way to this energy.

Most modern healers do not deny that doctors and hospital treatments play their part, and the very best spiritual healers are concerned to complement, rather than fight against, present-day medicine. They accept that in some cases drugs and surgery may be necessary, and that a spiritual healer can never entirely replace the trained doctor.

No healer, says Don Copland, Secretary of the National Federation of Spiritual Healers, is allowed to give a medical diagnosis, as this is against their code of conduct. 'We're not doctors,' he says, 'and we could easily misdiagnose, so we don't do it. Anyway, what's the point? We want to help doctors, not work against them.' But according to healers it is only beneficial energy, not medicines or drugs, that can make us truly well.

When a healer tunes into a patient, he or she acts as a conduit, a channel, for this healing energy to be transmitted to the sick person. Most healers would say that the gift of healing comes through them, rather than from them, and that for some reason they have been chosen to act as such channels.

What healing can and can't achieve

There can never be any guarantee that healing will bring about the miracle that medical science has failed to perform, although this does very often happen. In many cases on record – and not just in the Bible – the lame have walked, bent backs have straightened, tumours have vanished and chronic arthritis or allergy has disappeared. But no healer has yet been able to reverse Down's Syndrome, for instance, or cystic fibrosis.

Healers have been able to make the blind see and the deaf hear, but they cannot, simply by thought power, rebuild a face that had been smashed in a road accident.

Nor can healers postpone death infinitely. We all have to die, and sometimes healers see their job as easing the passage between life and death, to enable the patient to let go of this life without fear. Sometimes, too, healing works to help those who have to watch a sick person die, or to bring up a badly handicapped child. Or it can give the terminally or chronically ill a more positive attitude – an acceptance and serenity rather than resentment and anger.

Gail Childs had many problems when she first sought spiritual healing. A form of cancer known as Hodgkin's lymphoma had been diagnosed in 1979, and she was also suffering from agoraphobia. It was after she suffered a bereavement that she felt she really needed help.

She read an article about spiritual healing in the *Daily Mail,* and this prompted her to contact a healing clinic in Pinner, Middlesex, near where she lives. Gail, who now works as a receptionist at the clinic, says:

> *I'd never had anything to do with spiritual healing before, but felt I needed something more than the medical care I was getting – I had been having radiotherapy and chemotherapy for the cancer.*
>
> *At the very first session, I felt that something important was happening. I had a lovely feeling when the healers put their hands on my head and shoulders, but it took two or three sessions before I was really able to relax. Then I started to look forward to the sessions and felt a completely different kind of person. I saw the world through more positive eyes.*
>
> *The cancer is not cured, and I have to go every now and again for check-ups. But the doctors are very pleased that it's not progressing, and is not as bad as they thought it would be. Formerly I also had to see a psychiatrist about the agoraphobia, which has now completely gone, thanks to the healing.*
>
> *I'd recommend spiritual healing for anybody. Now that I work at the clinic, I can see such a huge difference in the patients. Most of them are completely unable to relax when they first come to the clinic, and this is actually one of the most important things the healers do – get patients to relax.*

Whatever healing is, it is not necessarily the same as making better, as we understand it. We have to understand that there are very many levels of illness, very many levels of wellness, and different kinds of healing. We could say that all healing works on the mental level, even when enormous physical changes have been effected. Although we must all die eventually, healers believe that the human body has an almost infinite capacity to get well, that tissues can be restored, organs regenerated and tumours dispersed when the healing energy bounds through the body and mind.

Healers on healing

Those who have discovered the gift of healing within themselves, usually completely by accident, have different ways of explaining exactly what it is . Don Copland, an engineer with his own business before retiring to be a full-time healer, says:

> *I regard healing, particularly the hands-on type of healing, as a kind of jump lead which enables people to start healing themselves. There is no doubt that miracles do occur, but by their very nature, they are rare.*
>
> *I had an arthritic patient once whose hands were so gnarled she had been advised to have her wedding ring cut off. This distressed her greatly, but she could not get it off any other way. But after healing, the swelling in her joints went down and she was able to get the ring off quite easily. When she first came to see me her arthritis was so bad that she had to hold a cup of tea in both hands. Even this she did with great difficulty. Her husband had to carry her in to see me – she couldn't even walk. But now she has improved so much that she goes ballroom dancing.*

The point about healing, according to Copland, is that it always works – on one level or another. Sometimes, this happens to the amazement of doctors and nurses in hospital. Don's own story bears this out.

> *In June 1989, I was in hospital for a ruptured aorta. The medical staff were brilliant, but I know that the reason I came out of hospital completely fit and healthy, against all medical predictions, was because lots of healers came to visit me. With this operation, only*

four out of every hundred patients recover within a year. Yet only weeks later I had completely recovered.

Don Copland is convinced that all physical and mental illness manifests itself to teach us some important lesson. Until that lesson has been learnt, we will have to keep getting ill in one way or another.

When I collapsed with the ruptured aorta, people said to me: 'You're supposed to be a healer. Why did something like this have to happen to you?' I think now that it was to give me a closer understanding of, and link with, the medical profession. The doctor in my case, who was amazed at my quick recovery, said that he realized I had help from a lot of spiritual healers, but asked me to give the medical profession a little bit of credit. In fact, the surgeon told me later he did not expect that I would ever get off the operating table. I was on a life-support machine for two days.

As it was, I had a six-hour operation and now have a plastic aorta. I also believe that I went down with this very serious illness to enable me to overcome my fear and phobia of hospitals and operations. I believe in reincarnation – as very many healers do these days – and I have learnt that in a previous life I was a surgeon before the days of anaesthetic. I caused great pain to people, and that is why, in this life, I have always been terrified of hospitals. I had to get rid of this fear before I could proceed as a full-time healer – and, of course, this major operation did the trick. My fear has now gone.

Copland says that he became a healer completely by accident, and very many members of the Federation would say the same.

My former wife Audrey (also now a healer) was suffering very badly from neck problems, and had to wear a collar. She was in agony, and didn't know what to do to relieve the pain. One night I put my hands on her head, and she said it was like an infra-red lamp being put there. The next morning she got out of bed and her neck, which had been locked into the upper part of her back, began to get better.

She had no more problems, even though the doctors had not been able to help her. It was this that started off my healing career, although at the time I had my own business and so I practised healing just with friends. All my friends and acquaintances were highly sceptical when they heard about my supposed healing abilities, and would come up to me saying, "Ha, ha, I've got a bad knee." Then I would put my hands on their knee and heal them. They were amazed.

I also found I could run my hands an inch away from someone's body and feel what was wrong with them, from the heat coming off from the affected part. In nine times out of ten, I would be right.

Basically, he believes, spiritual healers are helping people to restore their own energy balance. 'Our whole systems are run by energy,' he says.

Why do people want to become healers? Nowadays doctors, psychiatrists, nurses, social workers and others involved in medical care are eagerly booking places on the basic healing course run by the Federation. 'After all,' says Copland, 'What is a healer?'

Simply somebody who makes people whole. So many people nowadays come up to me and say: 'I wish I could heal.' My reply to them is: 'You can.' You can smile at a little old lady on the bus – that's a form of healing. You can send out loving messages as you pass by a hospital or a prison – that's a form of healing. You can make sure you think only positive thoughts about other people – that's healing, both for yourself and the other person. We should never underestimate the power of energy or vibrations in the universe. Just because we can't see vibrations, it doesn't mean they don't exist. . . .

I think more and more people are realizing that drugs and surgery are not always the answer. It's not drugs, though, that are in themselves causing the problems, but the overuse of drugs. It's wrong, as we see it, for doctors to prescribe more than two weeks' supply at a time.

The basic NFSH course lasts over two weekends, or there is an intensive course lasting three days. These courses concentrate on inducing a state of relaxation and freedom from tension, using specific breathing exercises to enable the body and mind to relax. After that come specialist courses on different aspects of healing such as using colour and crystals. 'I think people want to become healers because they wish to repay a debt,' says Don Copland. 'Most of our healers have been patients at one time or another, who have made what might be termed a miraculous recovery. This has made them want to help others on the road to health.'

Although modern spiritual healers must charge for their services, they should not seek fame or wealth. These pursuits will weaken their healing powers.

When working, visualization is essential. Healers must be able to visualize a flow of loving, peaceful energy coming into the body. This energy should be visualized as coming from the healer's higher self. Healers also have to visualize beautiful colours – rose pinks, deep blues, golden light – and warmth, love, peace filling the body and creating new energy.

Once the healer has visualized this energy, the next step is to imagine it being released through the mind, from the heart and hands, to the patient. The patient must then be seen in full health and strength, and not as an ill person. If you have a person before you in a wheelchair, for instance, you have to visualize them as up and walking, their paralysed limbs suffused with healing energy.

Healers must also be able to visualize both themselves and the patient in front of them being filled with beautiful light. When the session ends, healers have to 'ground' themselves by mentally disconnecting with the patient. By the time the patient goes out through the door, there must be complete separation.

Another well-known healer, the late Major Bruce McManaway, believed that healing is brought about mainly by the power of thought. As such, he said, it is a subtle form of communication between the patient and healer which accelerates the patient's own natural healing abilities. Healing is basically an interplay of energy, and is natural, rather than supernatural. It works, he said, regardless of whether the patient has 'faith', either in the healer, or in his or her personal ability to recover from the illness.

Modern experiments have shown that effective healers have distinctive brainwave patterns, similar to those found in genuine Eastern holy men. The most concerted research into this was conducted by the late Maxwell Cade, an electrical engineer who tested large numbers of healers to try and discover whether anything measurable was happening during a healing session. Cade, who studied medicine and clinical psychology at London University, discovered that very often the healer was able to induce an altered brainwave pattern in the patient, which helped to bring about the healing process. The alteration in brainwave patterns was demonstrated to the satisfaction of scientists and doctors on his Mind Machine, a device he developed with his colleague Geoffrey Blundell. Cade also found that the patient could not produce this altered brainwave without help from a healer. The tests that Cade and Blundell developed showed that the patient was more relaxed, and at the same time more wide awake, than formerly. There was a deep physical relaxation response, which had an immediate beneficial effect on health.

Relaxation has already proved to be of value in the non-spiritual healing field. Consultant cardiologist Dr Peter Nixon, of London's Charing Cross Hospital, has found that if heart patients can be helped to relax and become less tense, very often they do not need bypass surgery because their condition mends itself. Dr Nixon's method involves administering short-term tranquillizers under medical supervision. He is also a great believer in the therapeutic power of massage. But it must be said that he is virtually alone among cardiologists in his approach – most favour the more glamorous and high-tech bypass surgery.

It is very probable, said Bruce McManaway, that spiritual healing works to some extent on the placebo effect – in simple terms this means that the power of suggestion can actually set in motion the healing process. In other words, if you believe something works, then very likely it will work. This effect can be demonstrated in a number of contexts. In trials to investigate new drugs, many of the patients who are unknowingly given placebos, or dummy pills, will feel better or make some kind of recovery. And have you noticed how very often a newly prescribed or marketed drug seems to have an almost miraculous effect? Very often it will appear very much better than the old pills for the same problem. We are always hearing about new and more effective migraine tablets, new and more effective tranquillizers and anti-depressants. But after a few years, these drugs suddenly don't seem to be quite so wonderful. Their placebo effect has worn off. It's a case of new brooms sweeping clean. We can never underestimate the power of suggestion, not even with the most meticulously developed and researched high-tech drug.

But Bruce McManaway believed there is far more than placebo to spiritual healing. This, he said, has been demonstrated in many university laboratories in several countries. It has been revealed on encephelographs that healing can bring about profound changes in adults, children and animals; the fact that it very often works on animals should give us some indication that it is by no means 'all in the mind', McManaway said. In medical trials patients undergoing spiritual healing have often said that they have felt definite physical sensations: a common one is a feeling of heat in the affected areas. Other patients have reported that the sensation was as of a battery being recharged.

There is no general agreement among healers about exactly what it is they are harnessing, or tapping into, but they all agree that the healing power comes from some kind of energy outside themselves. Unlike doctors, it is not they who are healing, but something quite beyond them. Opinions differ as to what this 'something' is. For Christian healers it would of course be the power of God, Christ or the Holy Ghost. For Spiritua*list* healers (as opposed to spiritual ones) it could be their guide from the spirit world, a discarnate entity which they contact when in a trance.

Bruce McManaway said that, although we may not understand exactly what the healing 'energy' is, we must believe that the entire universe consists of energy pulsating at different rates. If we also believe in the second law of thermodynamics, which says that energy cannot be created or destroyed, only changed, it is not a very big step to believing that there is a great deal of energy available for us to utilize for our own benefit. With the help of effective healers, we can use this energy to bring about beneficial physical changes. McManaway believed that the healer's state of mind is important, as well. There must be no sense of ego, no idea that the healer is bringing about these changes, or the gift may disappear. This represents a major difference between healers and doctors. Many doctors who have achieved success in high-tech fields such as transplants and in vitro fertilization are extremely egotistical in this sense. They believe that they, by their own efforts, have effected a miraculous cure or treatment.

Although a spiritual healer does not use surgical instruments or drugs to achieve results, there are nevertheless tools which can be used to set the healing process in motion. One of the most famous of the new generation of spiritual healers, Matthew Manning, believes that there are four effective healing tools. These are: humour and laughter (increasingly being accepted as a way of inducing relaxation, relieving stress and enabling the healing process to swing into action); creative visualization, where the patients imagine themselves to be in complete health; correct breathing (this is also considered extremely important by Dr. Peter Nixon, who believes that very many serious chronic complaints are caused by hyperventilation, which results in the wrong mixture of carbon dioxide and oxygen getting to body and brain cells); and physical exercise.

Matthew Manning, along with many other healers, believes that a lot of illness in the modern world is caused by a combination of fear and over-seriousness. 'Whenever people are too serious,' he says, 'they create anxiety and tension. Whatever can work to break undue seriousness and opens us up to play and the natural child within us will bring about recreation and self-healing.'

Matthew says that when patients first arrive at the Matthew Manning Healing Centre – having very often been given up as hopeless by the medical profession – they usually have at least three things working against them: fear, isolation and depression. He explains: 'By allowing yourself to be frightened, isolated and depressed, you are effectively helping the process of the illness and reducing the efficiency of the body's ability to fight back.' Negativity, says Matthew, is the single biggest stumbling-block towards good health. The only real way to lasting health is to get to know ourselves, to come to an understanding of why we have become ill and of how we can get better by positive thinking and correct relaxation. Self-healing can only really take place when we can remove fear, anger, resentment and all negative attitudes, and replace them with humour and positivity.

Although no healer or doctor would advocate smoking, drinking and gambling as ways to health, the case of Jeffrey Bernard illustrates how somebody can continue to abuse their body and be almost on death's door, yet spring back and back and back, because of humour, positivity and a willingness not to take anything too seriously. Jeffrey Bernard, who was played first by Peter O'Toole and then by Tom Conti in the successful West End Play *Jeffrey Bernard Is Unwell,* has become famous for writing a 'Low Life' column in the *Spectator,* a column in which he philosophizes on life in general and his life in particular. It is highly amusing, mainly because Bernard laughs only at himself, not at other people – which is, of course, the secret of real humour. A person without humour is a person full of fear, and fear is the biggest health-destroyer there is.

An apparent discarnate entity who has helped many people is 'White Eagle', supposedly a long-dead Indian chief who has infinite wisdom and who was channelled over many years by Grace Cooke, co-founder with her husband Ivan of the White Eagle Lodge. White Eagle says that, in order to be healed, humans must see themselves as spirit rather than flesh. Once this is the case, everything else can be seen in a different, healthier perspective, and fear and anxiety start to vanish. White Eagle teaches that everything which exists in the universe is, whether we accept it or not, infused by spiritual essence. Without this, he says, nothing can exist. It is spiritual energy which gives living things their life. Without it, they are dead.

According to White Eagle, all successful healing must proceed on the understanding that we are more than bodies relying on somebody else – a doctor or nurse or therapist – to make us better. Most illness, at least most chronic illness, comes about because of the fear of death. If this could be removed, we would be a long way towards healing ourselves. Sickness will remain until we can think healthily and positively. Disease comes, says White Eagle, when physical cells are out of alignment, and the cause is always the same: we have lost touch with God, or the spiritual within ourselves. As all sickness has the same root cause, so is the power which heals always the same – it is the power of God. Fear, hate and resentment are just as much products of disharmony as are cancerous cells or arthritic fingers. We should also realize, White Eagle says, that all suffering has a purpose. Instead of asking 'Why me?' – a completely unanswerable question anyway – we should ask ourselves what we can learn of value from our illnesses. Once we have learned the lessons, we will not suffer from these illnesses again.

The way to self-healing

Self-healing can take a lot of hard work; it can involve not only altering our diet and lifestyle, but profoundly changing our attitudes to ourselves and those around us. If we want to be well we must understand the power of thought, and realize that by our thoughts we can bring about premature old age and many illnesses. If we have violent or angry or resentful thoughts, these will rebound on ourselves – not on our enemies. White Eagle says that universal laws operate on precise law and order, not luck and chance.

I once witnessed a dramatic example of the way hatred can kill when I worked at a particular Sunday newspaper. My boss, a very difficult woman, hated me, hated the rest of the staff, and, it seemed, just about all of humanity. Her hatred of everything was so great that she spent most of her time sitting in a darkened room, never going out for lunch or any other reason, and amassing large sums of money and consumer goods. Her office cupboards were full of 'free gifts' and samples which were never returned. Every Friday her husband used to come and meet her, and they would hump the week's haul home together. All the usual jokes about her husband having to hire National Carriers met with stony stares.

This went on for years, but eventually she started to be ill. First she developed fibroids; then she contracted cancer. Before long she died, at the early age of fifty, absolutely eaten up with rampant cancer. What caused that cancer apart from hatred?

In spiritual healing terms, we have to understand that all illness is the result of *karma* working itself out. This concept of *karma* – a Sanskrit word for which there is no useful English equivalent, unfortunately – means that for every action there will inevitably be a suitable reaction; as you sow, so shall you reap. If you become ill, this is inevitably the result of some bad *karma*, or action, you have done in the past. It is not, as some people imagine, a system of punishment and reward, but a direct consequence. (If you smoke eighty cigarettes a day, lung cancer is not a punishment but an inevitable result of the smoking. Your lungs have not been able to accommodate so much poison, and have packed up as a result; it is no use blaming anybody.) Most spiritual healers believe that, whenever illness manifests itself in the body or the mind, it is because some past *karma* has caused a serious imbalance. The problem may have started in a previous life, they say.

Now, if you were to go to an ordinary GP and say that you thought your present illness must be caused by past *karma*, he or she might think seriously about admitting you to a psychiatric ward. But the point is, for all their investigations and work, for all the medical advances that have been made, we are still very much a world of extremely sick people. And all the drugs, all the psychiatric care, all the alternative therapists are not materially lessening the amount of illness in the world. The most that the average doctor or therapist can do is to make people better for a while. Then, more than usually, they will get something else wrong with them. Healers would say that this is because the spirit is not healed, because attitudes have not changed, because old negative patterns of thinking are still intact.

If you want to be truly healed, say spiritual healers, you must be prepared to undertake hard work yourself. You must do your utmost to eradicate all negative or erroneous ways of thinking and relating to other people. You must, first and foremost, have love – love for yourself, love for the rest of humanity.

True healing, then, is the healing of body, mind and spirit by a combination of positive, loving attitudes, a responsibility towards the body – that is, not over-indulging in harmful food and drink – and, possibly, the infusion of something extra, variously called healing or divine energy, from a healer.

2 ❧ The Healers

A LONG HISTORY

Spiritual healing, becoming ever more popular today, goes back to the beginning of time. In early cultures, all healing was considered to be the work of spiritual forces. In Ancient Egypt and Greece, no distinction was made between healers and priests; religion and medicine were virtually synonymous, and all holy men and women would automatically be healers as well. That ability was, then as now, considered a very rare and precious gift, by no means given to all.

In addition, the ancients firmly believed that non-physical forces were involved in illness. There was never any suggestion that illness was merely bad luck, a matter of an invading germ, or just part of the mechanism going wrong. They were certain that evil spirits, or at the very least some serious disharmony between humanity and God, or divine forces, were the cause of bodily sickness. The idea that disease and sickness are merely malfunctions of mechanical parts is a modern premise – upon which most modern medicine is based.

Most Christians would probably say that the earliest and greatest spiritual healer was Jesus, and over the years countless millions of words have been written on his ability to heal the sick and perform miracles by the mere laying on of hands. But spiritual healing goes much further back than Christ. In pre-Christian times, yogis from the East could heal themselves and other people through meditation, prayer and ascetic practices.

The very first 'miracle' healer of whom we have records was the Egyptian Imhotep, who was both magician and physician at the court of King Zoser, in about 3000 BC. After his death Imhotep was deified, and would, according to legend, heal patients in their dreams.

The Greek physician Asklepios was also a wondrous healer and he too was deified after his death. He is the patron saint of all physicians and his emblem, a snake coiled round a rod, is the symbol of medicine today. After his death a major cult grew up around him, and he was said to be able to heal and perform operations, like Imhotep, through dreams.

Both the ancient Egyptians and the Greeks, in common with the Chinese, Indians and Tibetans, believed that all healing was ultimately spiritual healing. Unless spiritual forces were invoked, they maintained, no healing could take place. Both Pythagoras and Hippocrates mention 'healing energies' in their writings, and Plato said that the body cannot be healed without first paying attention to the soul. All ancient cultures without exception believed that it was impossible to separate the body from the soul.

But although all cultures had their miracle workers, Jesus Christ remains the most interesting of the ancients, if for no other reason than that his work and teachings still have a major impact today, while the works and writings of other contemporary or older healers are studied only by specialized historians and anthropologists. At the moment much of this ancient knowledge is being revived for popular consumption as interest in spiritual healing is growing: it seems increasingly as though things are coming full circle.

It does appear as though the healing miracles attributed to Jesus actually happened, and were not just written into the gospels centuries later by mythologizing scribes. Throughout his three-year ministry, Jesus regularly underlined the strength of his revolutionary teachings by a series of happenings which seemed to defy all natural laws – walking on water, turning water into wine, making the lame walk, curing lepers, raising the dead to life. Very many Christian commentators have attempted to explain the significance, in theological terms, of Jesus' healing miracles. For Robert Peel, a Christian Scientist who is also author of a number of scholarly books on spiritual healing, Christ's miracles were an 'integral part of a new order brought into effect by the Son of God'.

Jesus, Christian commentators tell us, viewed sickness very much as the enemy of humans, and saw its source as Satan, or evil. Through healing the sick, Christ defeated Satan and demonstrated the workings, and the possibility, of the Kingdom of God on earth. All sickness is caused by some kind of sin, according to this doctrine, and if sin can be made to vanish, then good health will be the result.

When Christianity was in its infancy, it was considered that healing was a true spiritual gift, and that anybody possessing this gift had truly been blessed by the Holy Spirit. In the second century AD healing work was performed by Christian bishops and priests, but by the fourth century the whole concept of spiritual healing had virtually died, and healing was no longer considered to be a part of the Christian ministry. Although Jesus demonstrated convincingly that healing miracles were possible, and instructed his apostles to go and heal the sick as he had done, this practice fell into disuse as soon as the Christian Church was firmly established.

Why was this? One explanation is that there was a deeply held fear that occult practices, Devil worship and witchcraft could easily be associated with healing, especially the type of healing which seemed to run counter to scientific laws. There is also, apparently, a long tradition of Christian thinking which says that major miracles stopped after the establishment of the Church because they were no longer needed. But when one thinks of the terrible plagues and scourges of the Middle Ages, this argument becomes nonsense. There has always been a great need for healing – but it has not always been available.

After the decline of spiritual healing, modern 'rational' medicine developed and it came to be believed that drugs and surgery could heal most diseases. Medicine moved to the material plane and the early connection with priests, magic and religion was forgotten as long training in medical schools became compulsory for those who wanted to set themselves up as healers. Unfortunately one of the results was some very bad medicine indeed: operations were performed in filthy conditions without anaesthetic, and most cures and treatments were cruel and painful. This has not actually stopped today –

it's just that general and local anaesthetics take away our perception of pain, and we have discovered the importance of hygiene. But modern hospitals are still places of illness, not of health and healing.

Theosophy

Towards the end of the nineteenth century, however, Helena Petrovna Blavatsky, the co-founder with Henry Olcott of the Theosophical Society, taught that the mind must be addressed if the body is to be well. Blavatsky, widely ridiculed and reviled in her day, wrote a number of books supposedly inspired from her Tibetan masters, or 'mahatmas', after she had reputedly spent a number of years in Tibetan monasteries. Theosophy, which was supposed to reconcile Eastern and Western religions and modes of thought, brought back the idea of the spiritual into the concept of sickness and disease. Its influence has been powerful, and many branches of present-day holistic medicine owe their formation to Theosophical ways of thinking.

Some Christians still believe that suffering and sickness are sent by God to teach us important lessons. The children's writer and Oxford don C.S. Lewis often declared that God used pain and sickness to break us of our rebellious natures; sickness, he said, is some kind of mortification or punishment. It should be emphasized that spiritual healers do not hold this view at all. They believe that sickness of the spirit is at the root of all illness, but not that disease is sent by God as a punishment for our wicked ways. In any case, C.S. Lewis' pronouncements were pure guesswork: he was not a healer himself, and had received, so far as is known, no divine revelations at all.

Apart from Theosophy, modern spiritual healing owes its resurgence to two other important nineteenth-century movements – Christian Science and spiritualism, both of which placed primary importance on the influence of the mind, or spirit, on the body. They also put healing back into its original religious context, and gave God, or divine laws, a central place. When they first became major movements in the West, spiritualism and Christian Science seemed to be operating in direct contradiction to the scientific, rational approach that medicine was increasingly taking. The practitioners of orthodox medicine said then, and still do say to a great extent, that humans are machines which occasionally go wrong, but which can be put right with the correct spanners, oil and engineering – that is, drugs and surgery.

Christian Science

Still a powerful movement today, particularly in America, Christian Science is based on the belief that spiritual healing is just as available to people nowadays as it was during Christ's ministry. For Christian Scientists, it is possible in the twentieth century to bring about healing miracles through prayer and a spiritual understanding of God.

The movement founded in 1875 by Mary Baker Eddy with the publication of the now famous *Science and Health,* was the first 'modern' doctrine which said that illness and disease were basically all in the mind, or at least that they originated in the mind, and that the only reality was spiritual, non-material. Mary Baker Eddy, an American housewife, suffered a severe accident and was not expected to live. But she made a total recovery while thinking about the New Testament healing miracles, and decided that the rest of her life would be devoted to studying the connection between healing and prayer. Christian Science has earned itself a probably undeserved reputation for believing that all pain is mental in origin, and that if you think and pray hard enough it will go away.

Briefly, Christian Science teaches that God is the creative principle behind all things, and that humanity is essentially good, well-intentioned and spiritual. The most important, permanent things are those of the spirit, while matter and material things are only temporary, an illusion, insubstantial, not basically worth bothering about. So we should strive first and foremost to improve our spiritual selves and not worry overmuch about amassing wealth or material objects. Once we can learn to do this, we shall become well and free from disease, as we will then be living according to the tenets of the New Testament as expounded by Christ.

The First Church of Christ, Scientist, was established in 1892 in Boston, Massachussetts, and has grown to become an international organization with around four thousand churches in fifty or more countries. There are no ordained clergy as such; all full-time Christian Scientists devote themselves to the healing ministry, and election of officers is by democratic vote and rotation. The movement is responsible for the *Christian Science Monitor,* a well-respected daily newspaper with an international following, read by many non-Christian Scientists.

Robert Peel, one of the movement's best-respected commentators and author of many books on Christian Science, maintains that spiritual healing is enjoying a major revival just now because we are at last realizing that we cannot be free of sickness and disease unless we accept that we have a spiritual as well as a physical aspect. He says that when we pray effectively for healing we are tapping into the spiritual world, which is part of the natural order of things. All kinds of faith, such as faith in doctors, psychotherapists, acupuncturists and other therapists, may contribute to healing, but it is only an unshakeable faith in God which can transcend the apparent laws of nature. (This actually contradicts what many non-Christian Science spiritual healers say, which is that the sick person does not need any personal faith in order to be effectively healed.)

Modern medicine, says Peel in his book *Spiritual Healing in a Scientific Age,* rests almost completely on the concept of a human being as a 'physical organism shaped by the interaction of chance and law through eons of development'. This approach, he states, has resulted in medicine causing at least as much sickness as it cures. The major writer on this subject is Ivan Illich (not a Christian Scientist), who coined the term 'iatrogenic' to describe illnesses which have been brought about directly through medical intervention.

The march of orthodox medicine, Peel tells us, has brought about many needless operations, dangerous side-effects of drugs, resistant strains of bacteria developed through overuse of antibiotics, diseases brought about by antitoxins and the confusion of the temporary placebo effect of a new drug with the supposed curative power attributed to it.

Intensive care units, Peel says, produce diseases and also sick states such as insomnia, fear and anxiety, and most people assume there is far more science in medicine than there actually is; in fact, it proceeds pretty much by guesswork and by using humans as guinea pigs for new drugs and treatments. In addition the record of success is startlingly low, given how much faith we currently have in orthodox medicine. Many modern doctors believe that more and better research grants, more hospitals, doctors and nurses, are all that we need to improve our health. But one can say with complete certainty that in fifty years of the most intensive cancer research possible, with millions of pounds spent annually, we are no nearer either prevention or a cure. In fact many types of cancer are on the increase.

It is because of all this, because more of us are realizing that the medical emperor has very few clothes, that people are once again turning towards spiritual healing. It is one of the most important aspects of Christian Science teachings that its members should show their faith by healing the sick, and also themselves. 'Love', says Robert Peel, 'may be a more exact instrument than chemical analysis or genetic experimentation.' Christian healing, by contrast with medical intervention, draws its power from the 'deep wellsprings of spiritual perception'.

In order to be a successful spiritual healer, according to Peel, spiritual commitment and discipline are necessary. As with any important skill, study and practice are needed. 'Christian healing is not for credulous dabblers', he says.

Most present-day Christian Scientists do not have much time for orthodox medicine and rely almost completely on spiritual healing. The real task of Christian Scientists, according to Mary Baker Eddy, is to heal the world from sin. Healing sickness and disease is only an interim measure, necessary while there is so much illness in the world.

Whereas most spiritual healers are nowadays trying their utmost to work with, rather than against, the medical profession, Christian Science has no such intention. This movement says that there can be no real marriage between effective Christian Science and conventional medicine: the two cannot work in unison. Nor do Members of the movement accept that their type of healing is one more branch of alternative medicine, but say that it is a complete way of life in itself which acknowledges the supremacy of the spirit.

For this reason, Christian Science healers have always been reluctant to take part in controlled trials with doctors or researchers. This, of course, gives the opposition much needed ammunition, and they can say it's all nonsense, trickery, placebo or fakery. The reason for the reluctance, says Robert

Peel, is the uncertainty factor: events and personalities affect the outcome of any experiment. In fact, quantum physics says that the presence of the person conducting the experiment will always affect the outcome. But in the meantime, the assertion that Christian Science works does little to convince the Doubting Thomases.

Most doctors are still extremely sceptical about Christian Science, but there are many cases on record of people recovering from serious illness. Betty Louise Brunn's youngest son John, for instance, was born in November 1946 with seriously deformed feet. Doctors said that he would never be able to walk as he was double club-footed and one heel had no joint. It was, the doctors said, a congenital deformity. But Betty, a devout Christian Scientist, refused to accept the doctor's prognosis. She asked a Christian Science practitioner to pray for John, and she herself also prayed for the complete healing of her son. At fifteen months he began to walk, and by the age of three there was nothing at all wrong with his feet. At school, John became a keen baseball player and later joined the Air Force – a rigorous medical showed that there was no trace of deformity in either of his feet.

Kathryn Ashby's son Roderick was involved in a serious car accident at the age of five. He suffered concussion and several broken bones. Kathryn asked permission to rely completely on Christian Science for the child's recovery. The doctors were concerned and advised surgical setting of the shoulder. Kathryn refused, and in two weeks Roddy was completely healed, without any stitches or conventional medical care.

Spiritualism
Like Christian Science, spiritualism places great emphasis on healing in its work. Most spiritualist churches hold healing sessions, and people flock to professional spiritualists at their headquarters in Belgrave Square, London, for both contact and absent healing. Spiritualists differ from Christian Scientists in that, although both believe in a basically benevolent God and universe, the former believe that healing occurs through channelling of spirit guides – discarnate entities on the ethereal plane who are full of wisdom and compassion. The mediums who preside at spiritualist healing services regard themselves simply as channels for the healing energy.

Not all spiritual healers by any means are spiritualists, but in common with the spiritualist healers they regard themselves as channels. Some believe they are channelling a discarnate entity, while others see themselves as conduits for healing energy. Spiritualist healing will be examined more fully on p. 90, since it has developed into a separate form of healing in its own right.

Healers in the twentieth century

During this century, a remarkable collection of spiritual healers of all kinds has emerged thoughout the world. In Africa, America, Britain, the Philippines and Australia, healers without medical qualifications, often working without charging and in extremely primitive conditions, have been performing what look very much like modern miracles.

BRITISH HEALERS

Harry Edwards

It was really Harry Edwards more than anybody else who in the twentieth century re-established spiritual healing as a major phenomenon. Born in 1893, Edwards discovered by accident that he had the gift of healing people without medical intervention. He developed this until, at the height of his fame in the 1950s and 1960s, he was filling the Albert Hall, Trafalgar Square and other large venues. He became convinced through his work that spiritual healing genuinely worked, and that he had an important message for the medical profession.

Huge sums of money, he felt, were being completely wasted in looking for treatments and cures, particularly for diseases such as cancer. Edwards, who claimed only a 20 per cent failure rate, believed that it was completely possible for the patient to use his or her own thoughts and emotional processes to be healed from cancer.

To further the work of spiritual healing, in 1955 he founded the National Federation of Spiritual Healers and became its first President. Unlike the Christian Scientists, Edwards was more than willing for his work to be fully investigated by the medical profession, and on several occasions he campaigned vigorously for this to be done. Yet it never came about, even though he was displaying powers that by any definition could be considered remarkable. It was also due to Edwards' tireless campaigning that in 1977 the British Medical Association withdrew their former ruling which had forbidden medically qualified people to send patients to healers; previously, they had only done so at the risk of being struck off. It is largely thanks to the pioneering work of Harry Edwards, and his refusal to admit defeat in the face of total indifference and opposition, that in Britain it is perfectly permissible for doctors to refer patients to healers, which they are now doing more and more. (In other countries, this is not the case. In the USA, for instance, it is only permissible to practise as a healer if one is also a member of a recognized religion. One of the resulting problems is that many so-called healers in America have set up their own religions, often with disastrous consequences.)

In addition to his public meetings, which drew crowds of thousands, Harry Edwards established his own healing sanctuary at Burrows Lea, in Surrey. Around five thousand letters a week were received there from sick people all over the world. The healing sanctuary still continues, now run by Joan and Ray Branch. Harry, who died in December 1976, kept all his cases on record, and was happy to give full information about his healing to anybody who asked for it. Here is one typical example of his success.

Jayne Smith was a teenager living in Lichfield, Staffordshire. She had extensive cancer of the left upper leg, could no longer walk, and the surgeons involved had been planning amputation as the only possible treatment. Detailed examination, however, showed that the cancer was too advanced even for this drastic measure. Jayne was not expected to live beyond a year, at most.

Her parents told their local rector, who took the family to Harry's healing sanctuary. When she arrived, Jayne's leg was as solid as wood; within a month of receiving healing, however, it had started to soften. Edwards continued to give Jayne spiritual healing, and maintained contact at other times by sending out absent healing. Within six months of this treatment, but no other, all the symptoms of cancer had disappeared and Jayne was walking and joining in activities with her school friends. On examining her, the doctors at the local hospital found that all the cancerous cells had been replaced by healthy tissue.

Bruce McManaway

It was during the Second World War that Bruce McManaway, who died in 1988, discovered to his surprise and astonishment that he could ease pain and help the wounded simply by the laying on of hands and sympathetic touch. He had no formal medical qualifications of any kind, but came to believe that we all have a little of the healer within ourselves.

Major McManaway was able to trace his gift back to an exact date – May 1940, when his army unit was suffering from a severe shortage of medical facilities. McManaway began putting his hands on the wounded and found that they often responded. He also noticed there were definite reactions in his patients: there was frequently a change of temperature, observable even when he was just in the vicinity. Where possible, McManaway used the laying on of hands technique, but sometimes soldiers were too badly wounded to be touched. At these times, McManaway would pass his hands over the wound – and the temperature change still took place. The wounded themselves would often report a tingling feeling.

As time went on, McManaway's healing gift became more pronounced and he could often, by using his hands, diagnose where pieces of shrapnel were buried in soldiers' bodies. He was usually accurate, as was confirmed later by doctors.

After the war, McManaway stayed on in the army as a career soldier, retiring in 1959. His healing gift remained, and he would often help fellow officers and soldiers, particularly those plagued by back trouble. McManaway decided to concentrate mainly on this region of the body, and came to believe that a very great deal of illness was located in the spine. The back, he said, is the 'central pipeline' for the nervous system, and so any imbalance is likely to be felt in this area. Every deep-seated emotional problem, McManaway believed, had a physical counterpart in the spine. After retiring from the army, he set himself up as a full-time healer and established the Westbank Healing and Teaching Centres in Scotland and London.

McManaway believed, like other spiritual healers, that we must first address the spirit if we are to be truly well. In order to understand his gift as fully as possible, he carefully researched the spiritual aspects of sickness and disease, and said that his gift worked by being able to feel whether there were blocked energies in the body. In this way, his kind of healing had much in common with acupuncture. He felt that healers do not need to have any specific medical knowledge in order to sense blocked energies and help to release them. Modern spiritual healers, though, are not allowed by their National Federation to diagnose.

McManaway, like so many spiritual healers, was certain that there exists a discarnate world and that we may obtain help from this world if we are correctly attuned to it. He likened the gift of healing to having one's own telephone installed, rather than having to use a public phone box. But, he said, although genuine healers will always have a link with the world of the spirit, sometimes the telephone will not be in good working order or there may be a fault on the line. He maintained that healing was not a complete substitute for medical skills and that good healers will seek not to supplant doctors, but to work in conjunction with them.

M.H. Tester

Maurice Tester was a successful property consultant and chartered surveyor who in middle age decided to take up golf. Soon, however, he developed agonizing backache and in 1959 a very bad case of prolapsed disc was diagnosed; doctors feared that he might well lose his leg. He had, it seemed, ruptured a disc between the fourth and fifth lumbar vertebrae, and serious complications had set in. Tester spent months trussed up in surgical jackets, went into traction and took hundreds of painkilling tablets. Nothing, it seemed, could touch the pain or mend the rupture.

A series of X-rays taken after months of ineffective treatment suggested that there might be some slight hope if he had a major operation. Instead, on the recommendation of a client, he decided to go and see a healer, Ted Fricker, who lived in Tottenham, North London, and had established a successful healing sanctuary there. Tester felt by this stage that there was nothing to lose, although he did not hold out much hope of the healer being able to do anything for him.

Fricker asked Tester to remove the spinal jacket he now wore constantly, and on doing so he immediately felt a lessening of the pain. This pleasant sensation was accompanied by one of sheer bewilderment, as after two years of agony, frustration and discomfort he felt relief for the first time. He could hardly believe it. After six weeks of intensive healing Tester's spinal problems had completely disappeared and he was perfectly all right.

Tester's doctor could offer no explanation at all for the sudden healing, but confirmed that it could not have come about by natural remission. Tester then returned to his healer and asked him to tell him precisely how it had all happened. Fricker told Tester that his power to heal came directly from God: he heard voices and followed their directions.

Then, Fricker told Tester the most amazing news: 'You're a healer, too', he said. 'You can do for others what I have done for you.'

Maurice Tester felt certain that something extraordinary had happened to him. He had been in agony; now he was cured. And more than that, here was somebody telling him that he too had healing powers. At any rate, Tester felt confident enough to give up his profession and become a full-time healer.

He came to feel, like Ted Fricker, that he was being guided by those in the spirit world for his healing work. He joined Hannen Swaffer's Home Circle, a group of people who met regularly to discuss psychic and supernatural phenomena.

Hannen Swaffer was a famous tabloid journalist of his day who, on behalf of his newspaper, had embarked on an investigation of mediums and psychic phenomena, with the intention of exposing it all as fraud and trickery. Instead, he became converted.

Tester came to feel that he was in touch with a band of spirit healers headed by the renowned Greek physician Galen. Most of the people who came to him, he wrote in his book *The Healing Touch,* were those with a long history of pain and suffering. They were, as he had been, at the end of their tether and had often been given up by the medical profession. Tester's observation was that those who had experienced most illness and disease in their lives were those most likely to be cured. After that, he said, their life was changed for ever. 'If you fill your body with pills and powders, it becomes incapable of spiritual self-prescription' he wrote.

Maurice Tester reckoned that the sick people who came to see him fell into two main categories – those who wanted to enjoy life, and those for whom every scrap of enjoyment had disappeared. The latter category could rarely be helped, he found, but so long as there was some capacity for enjoyment, there was hope. Tester also soon discovered from his work that happiness and optimism can create an environment in which the body can respond and become well again. Positive thinking was the main ingredient, he felt, to lasting health and wellbeing.

But sometimes, Tester discovered, the body has become too weak to sustain permanent improvement: there is always a limit, even for a spiritual hea᠎ r. But, he was careful to point out, spiritual healing has nothing to do with blessings or pronouncements from priests of orthodox religions. 'The blessings of priests or rabbis have no effect,' he wrote. Instead, spiritual healing means healing by somebody who is in direct touch with the spirit world, a place where there is greater refinement, wisdom and optimism than on this earthly plane. Maurice Tester died in 1986.

George Chapman

One of the most famous spiritual healers of modern times, George Chapman claims to channel the late ophthalmic surgeon Dr William Lang, who takes over Chapman's body to perform 'spirit operations' on the 'spirit body' of the sick person. Chapman, born in 1921, works from his headquarters at Machynlleth in Wales and also holds clinics in France and Switzerland. He has treated very many famous people, including Elvis Presley and the actor Laurence Harvey by 'absent healing'.

Chapman, who was born in Liverpool, led an ordinary life until the end of the Second World War, during which he served in the Royal Air Force. He had been a garage hand, professional boxer, butcher and docker, and after the war became a fireman, settling in Aylesbury, Buckinghamshire. In 1944 he married and the following year a daughter, Vivian, was born. She only lived for a month, and her father was heartbroken. In his autobiography *Surgeon from Another World,* as told to Roy Stemman, Chapman describes how he went into the woods and wept bitterly after Vivian's death, wondering why her life on earth should have been so very short.

Vivian's untimely death started him thinking about the

afterlife. To while away the time between calls the firemen at Chapman's station started dabbling in spiritualism, using a home-made ouija board. Soon, it seemed, they were contacting Red Indian and ancient Chinese spirits, but before long somebody rather different came through during the sessions. This was Dr William Lang, a distinguished eye surgeon who was born in 1852 and died in 1937. Lang revealed that he wished to continue his work on earth and had chosen George Chapman to be his main instrument.

Chapman, intrigued, began to investigate Lang's identity and credentials, and found that everything which was coming through was correct. At the same time Chapman discovered that he was able to go into trance, and at the age of twenty-five started his healing work, using Dr Lang as the spirit surgeon. By 1956, Chapman's healing work had progressed sufficiently to enable him to retire from his job and take up healing full-time.

What happens, says Chapman, is that his body and hands are taken over by Dr Lang to perform operations. The spirit body, he explains in *Surgeon from Another World,* is an exact double to the physical body, and contains spirit replicas of the same organs. If a tumour develops in the physical body, this will be paralleled in the spirit body. Altogether, Chapman explains, we have three bodies – the physical, the spirit and the etheric. The etheric, composed of electrical cells held together by a magnetic force, clings to the physical body and acts as a kind of messenger between the spirit and the physical bodies. Chapman says that he does not know what is going on when Dr Lang 'operates'. After falling into a trance, he begins to dream and knows nothing of the condition of the patients who come into his clinics. The credit is entirely due to Dr Lang, he says.

The modern, sceptical, rational reader may find all this very hard to take, especially as pictures of George Chapman show him 'operating' using his hands to manipulate invisible instruments. But it cannot easily be dismissed as complete nonsense. For one thing, Dr William Lang did really exist, and all the information relayed to Chapman apparently by Lang was later confirmed by his daughter Lyndon. Also, George Chapman had never heard of Dr Lang until the apparent spirit began to contact him.

Furthermore, very many of the operations have been highly successful and hundreds of people have been completely healed after their doctors had given up all hope. One of the most startling cases is that of journalist J. Bernard Hutton, who died in 1981. Hutton had suffered from poor eyesight all his life, and in 1963 began to go blind; he was in despair, because he thought he would no longer be able to work. He contacted many doctors and specialists, but without success. Then his wife read an article in *Psychic News* about a man living in Aylesbury who was having great success in treating people with eye problems,under guidance from a famous doctor from the spirit world.

Hutton decided he had nothing to lose, so wrote to George Chapman and received a reply that Dr Lang would see him. Chapman, speaking as Dr Lang, told him a lot about his eye condition, and also that he had hepatitis. Chapman appeared, wrote Hutton in his account of the phenomenon, *Healing Hands,* to be completely taken over by Dr Lang, who informed Hutton that he would operate on the 'spirit body' and attempt to produce a parallel effect in the physical body.

Hutton describes in his book how he experienced the physical sensations of incisions being made, despite the fact that the process was actually painless. Dr Lang was operating with invisible instruments above the physical body, Hutton learned. When Lang had finished, Hutton experienced the sensation of wounds being stitched up. As he was 'stitching up' the wounds, Dr Lang, speaking through George Chapman, told Hutton that if the hepatitis was not attended to shortly, the eye operations would not be of much use. He then attempted to extricate the offending virus in another spirit operation. All the time, Chapman's hands hovered above Hutton's body, looking as though they were holding instruments. Again, Hutton experienced strange painless sensations, as if a needle was being inserted, drawn out and then reinserted.

After it was all over, Hutton was asked to sit up and was horrified to discover that he could not see at all. Chapman, still speaking in Lang's voice, told him that there was in fact a considerable improvement, which would be noticed shortly. Hutton was also told that his condition had deteriorated so far that he could not expect to have absolutely normal eyesight ever again – but that he would be able to see.

Hutton then had a splitting headache. After the 'operation' he went to his car, still not being able to see at all. His wife had driven him down to Aylesbury, as by this time Hutton could not see well enough to drive. As he sat in the car, he noticed that gradually shapes were becoming discernible. He made out the shape of a tree, then noticed the car windscreen. He describes in *Healing Hands* how he wept as his sight gradually came back to him. There was no doubt, he said, that he could see far better than before. The terrible headache vanished as quickly as it had come, and all the aches and pains associated with the liver condition disappeared as well.

Hutton was then filled with an enormous sense of wellbeing. But he was still not convinced that anything 'real' had happened. He thought it must be all in his mind, and that by the next day his eyesight would start to deteriorate again. But to his amazement, that night, when he undressed for bed, he found that there was a long pink scar in the region of his liver, where 'Dr Lang' had performed the hepatitis operation.

He had gone to Aylesbury, he wrote, as a complete sceptic. Now he wasn't sure. But as the days and weeks went by, there was no doubt at all that his eyesight had improved considerably. So then, intrigued, Hutton began to investigate spiritual healing, George Chapman and Dr Lang. After exhaustive enquiries he became convinced that Chapman was completely genuine and that Lang had definitely existed; he could find no other explanation of the phenomenon but that Dr Lang, now in the spirit world, was actually performing these operations through George Chapman's physical body. Orthodox doctors, of course, dismissed it all as the power of suggestion, and put Hutton's recovery down to the placebo effect.

When he decided to write a book about his experiences, Hutton asked Chapman if he could contact Dr Lang for him to ask him how it was done. Speaking through Chapman, Lang explained that it all happened through the use of healing vibrations, which were exactly the same as those used by Jesus to perform his healing miracles.

Healing power, explained Lang, is drawn from the spirit world, although most conventional doctors will not accept such a thing. Dr Lang said that, as a spirit, he could see many things which would be invisible to other doctors, as they were concerned only with the materialistic plane. Their earthly conditions and cares actually hinder their sincere wish to heal, and put limitations on their abilities. Lang could, he said, see auras around people (which most doctors could not), and these auras told him exactly what was wrong with any particular patient because they change colour and look pale and grey when diseased.

Spirit surgery, Dr Lang said, is just the same as standard medical treatment, and it is not necessary to have faith or to believe in the supernatural or spirit world for it to work. The only thing that is vital, explained Dr Lang, is the patient's sincere wish to get better. Very many people build a whole lifestyle round being ill, and their illness gives them a sense of importance and specialness that they might not be able to enjoy if they were in good health. Such people – and among the chronically sick they are numerous – cannot be helped by spiritual healing.

Leah Doctors

George Chapman is not apparently the only healer of modern times who has been able to channel a medically qualified person from the spirit world. Leah Doctors was born in 1913 of Russian parents who came to London when she was a small girl. From the age of eight, Leah seemed to possess a healing gift, and later attended seances where she got in touch with a spirit guide, White Feather. As her family was poor, Leah had to leave school early and take a job in a tailor's shop. While working there, she gave spiritual healing to her employer, Mr Soskin. After this, she received a call from a new spirit guide, 'Dr Chang', supposedly a Chinese physician who had lived over five hundred years earlier.

After Leah contacted Dr Chang she gave up her tailoring work and, now married, established with her husband a healing sanctuary in London, which she later moved to Brighton. Dr Chang worked with 'healing rays' and, like Dr William Lang, conducted spirit operations on the spirit body. Leah Doctors came to specialize in healing diabetics and apparently enjoyed quite a lot of success.

In 1965 her work formed part of a *Whicker's World* programme, in which TV journalist Alan Whicker investigated fringe medicine, as it was then called. Later, in 1972, the TV programme *Man Alive* took up the subject. But Leah suffered a serious setback when a *News of the World* reporter, Michael Litchfield, decided to investigate the claims she was making for being able to diagnose and treat appendicitis.

Litchfield went to her complaining of pains in his side; Doctors (a highly suitable surname, one might think) instantly diagnosed it as acute appendicitis, and called on Dr Chang to perform the requisite spirit operation. So far so good – except that Litchfield's appendix had been removed twenty-seven years earlier! Another setback occurred when Joe Hutton, whose eyesight had been miraculously cured by Dr Lang, found that Leah Doctors could not help his wife.

There is no doubt, though, that Doctors, who has now passed into the spirit world herself, did help very many people with diabetes and other chronic complaints. Like George Chapman, she never made any claims or guarantees of success, and there seems little doubt that *something* happened around these people – although exactly what that is depends on your beliefs.

Betty Shine

Now in her sixties, Betty Shine is a well-known British spiritual healer who has been consulted by celebrities such as Michael Aspel, Michael Bentine and Michael Crawford. Betty, like most spiritual healers, says that she can sense the aura around people, and that she heals the spirit rather than the body. She can sense, she says, when somebody is healthy and positive, or depressed, negative and anxious.

She works from a bungalow in East Sussex with her partner Alan and her daughter Janet, also a medium. (It is common for mediumship and clairvoyance to run in the family: George Chapman's son Michael is also a healer, and channels Basil Lang, Dr William Lang's son, also a surgeon.) Betty, a clairvoyant, heals children, adults and animals who have been given up by the medical or veterinary professions. As with other healers, she does not guarantee miracles, and makes it clear that in many cases the illness will have gone too far for complete healing. Sometimes her task will be to help the very ill person die peacefully. George Chapman says that Dr Lang also sees this as part of his healing work – to ease the passage through to the next world.

As a child Betty Shine wanted to be a vet; instead, having married at nineteen a musician who encouraged her, she became an opera singer for twenty years. Then, at forty-six, Betty embarked on a new career as a healer. It happened when she went to see a clairvoyant who told her she was now ready to use her own healing gifts. She had been hearing voices for some time, and dismissed them as rubbish, but eventually heeded them and set up as a full-time healer from her home.

Betty, who never advertises, sees patients at her home and also, like all other spiritual healers, performs absent healing for those who are too ill to make the journey. George Chapman also sets great store by absent healing, and states that the healing takes place as soon as healing messages are sent out. Betty finds that absent healing works as well for animals as for humans. Another absent healer of pets, Sylvia Crystal Broadwood of London, has many testimonials from vets to say that the animals improved considerably after absent healing. Betty Shine says: 'I send a laser beam of healing light to animals, and very often they respond.' Plants, too, recover when Betty gives them healing. But, she says, her work does not mean that we do not need conventional medicine. The best gift that healers such as herself can give is that of positivity. Unless we have that, she says, we will never be well.

Sue Mckay, a management consultant, went to see Betty after she had contracted serious cancer in her early forties. Doctors said they could do no more for her, as this was the third cancer outbreak in her reproductive organs. She had already undergone extensive radiotherapy and chemotherapy and felt she could not stand any more, but would try to combat it through the power of the mind. She went to see Betty every two weeks for three months, and began to improve. Her doctors have now pronounced her completely clear of cancer.

Matthew Manning

No investigation of present-day British healers would be complete without a word or two about Matthew Manning. Known as Britain's most extensively tested healer (the scientific investigations on him will be described more fully in Chapter 3), Matthew was the subject of peculiar poltergeist activity while a teenager at boarding school. Such strange phenomena happened around the young Manning that he decided to harness this peculiar gift and become a full-time healer. He now has a thriving business selling books, tapes and videos, and makes national and international tours to talk about and demonstrate his work. In common with other healers, Matthew tends to see people whom the medical profession have given up as incurable.

Most of the healers mentioned so far have been uneducated, working-class, or at least middle-aged by the time they discover in themselves the healing gift. Matthew Manning is different on every count. He was born into an educated middle-class background, sent to private schools and developed his gifts while still in his early twenties.

AMERICAN HEALERS

Spiritual healers have proliferated in the USA even more than in Britain. Many have attracted a great deal of attention, some have made enormous fortunes for themselves, and yet others have been debunked by newspapers or the arch-exposer, magician and tracker-down of faith healers, James Randi. However, the fact is that spiritual healing is as much of a phenomenon on both sides of the Atlantic – and in both Britain and America there have been a number of remarkable people whose work and achievements cannot be explained by any ordinary means. Perhaps the most amazing healer of all, because he seems so absolutely genuine and has so far proved impossible to expose, was Edgar Cayce.

Edgar Cayce

Cayce was the first internationally known twentieth-century healer. His work, like that of so many others in the field, seems to go against all known scientific laws. Born in 1877 into a devout Christian family, he acquired at an early age a remarkable ability to learn things while asleep.

When he was twenty-one, and working as a salesman in a stationery store, he was troubled by a throat complaint which made talking difficult. He sought the advice of doctors, but none of them could find anything wrong; so he decided to try and help himself. Knowing that he had always possessed this ability to learn things while asleep, he asked a friend, Dr Layne, to suggest cures to him while he slept.

This treatment proved completely successful and led Cayce into a lifelong career as a spiritual healer. Known as the 'sleeping prophet', he was able to diagnose people's complaints and suggest cures even at great distances. Some years later the local newspaper, the **Bowling Green Times** of Kentucky, wrote a report of this ability, headlined: 'Bowling Green Man is Able to Diagnose Human Ills. Has No Recollection of It When He Awakes and Does Not Pretend to Understand His Wonderful Power.'

The first indication of his psychic powers came about two years after his self-cure from his throat problem, when Dr Layne asked if the young Cayce, now aged twenty-three, could psychically diagnose a very difficult medical condition that he himself had been unable to treat. Cayce diagnosed Dr Layne's patient's condition by going into a trance, and in this state, 'examined' the patient's body. Dr Layne asked him where the diseased organs were, and Cayce told him that there were extensive blood clots, disease in one of the lungs, and other signs of disease in the body. Cayce had no medical knowledge, did not know the patient, had never seen him, and had no idea what was wrong; he made his diagnosis by clairvoyant means of some kind.

As Cayce got older, his ability to diagnose diseases without the patient being physically present grew and grew. He himself had no idea of the source of his gift, and on one or two occasions decided to stop using them for healing. But he was always prevailed upon to try and diagnose and treat difficult conditions which defied medical treatment. In 1920 he and a friend, David Kahn, thought that the gift might be used to find oil wells in Texas – but this venture was not successful. Cayce had hoped to use the money he made from divining oil wells to finance a hospital dedicated to the diagnosis and treatment of apparently incurable illnesses.

Then Cayce started giving 'life readings' – the aspect of his work for which he became most famous – in which he began talking, again in trance, of the karmic reasons for people's illnesses and disease states. Karma, the Sanskrit word for action refers to the laws of cause and effect which state that you are born into the conditions you have created for yourself in a previous existence. Thus, in karmic terms, a child born with a serious handicap or illness would have 'earned' this through a previous existence. Cayce had no philosophical training at all, nor had he studied Eastern religions, which all encompass the idea of karma, and yet he was able to tell people of their previous incarnations, and why their previous life was adversely affecting their health in this particular existence. Of course, in order to take on board the idea of karma one has to accept the reality of reincarnation, and this at first Cayce was unwilling to do, coming as he did from a strong Christian background. But on studying the Bible he found that there were many references to reincarnation, and believed Jesus' famous saying: 'As you sow, so shall you reap,' was in fact referring to reincarnation.

Nowadays most, if not all, spiritual healers accept the idea of reincarnation, believing that many illnesses are caused by past karma intruding into this life. Cayce became far more than a healer of physical or even mental ills: while in trance he was able to tell thousands of people how they could use their past lives to achieve health and happiness in this incarnation. His thousands of readings, all now available in book form to those who are interested, cover all aspects of medicine and therapy, both orthodox and alternative, astrology, history, cosmology, sociology, geology, geography and a huge range of modern human problems. Whenever possible, Cayce tried to corroborate through scholars, encylopaedias and other reference books, the information he had received while asleep. It all matched up. Even nowadays, medical doctors are still astonished at the accuracy of Cayce's diagnoses and suggestions for treatment from one who had never studied medicine or pharmacology.

Professor I.C. Sharma, of Cleveland State University, a native of India and from a Hindu background, has carefully examined all the Cayce readings. He has come to the conclusion that Cayce's sleep state was one in which the human psyche, or soul, makes contact with cosmic consciousness and gains knowledge unlimited by time or space. Usually, says Professor Sharma in his book *Cayce, Karma and Reincarnation,* this state comes about with years of practice in meditation, and spiritual self-disciplines. With Cayce, though, since it was spontaneous, it must have been the 'result of the accumulated tendencies of previous incarnations'.

Rolling Thunder

An American Indian, chief of the Cherokee and Shoshone tribes, Rolling Thunder has demonstrated a remarkable ability to heal mental and physical illness. In 1971 he was a leading speaker at a major conference at which eighty-five doctors had gathered to talk about the connection between mind and illness.

One observer, Doug Boyd, recalls that Rolling Thunder walked down the aisle carrying an old suitcase, his 'doctor's bag', and went up to one of the delegates who was suffering from a serious leg injury. He addressed the four points of the compass as he breathed out, and then asked the patient whether he sincerely wanted to be healed from his condition. 'Do you just want to feel better?' asked the Indian chief, 'or what are you going to do? Is there anything else you would like to improve or change? Whatever you say now, that is the way it is going to be.'

Then the patient lay on his back as Rolling Thunder began a weird chant. He vomited into a basin several times, and began rubbing his hands together. He removed a feather from his hatband and with this (the commentary does not disclose whether Rolling Thunder was dressed in traditional Red Indian Costume) made long, sweeping movements over the patient's body. Finally he shook the feather at a piece of raw meat in his bag. Rolling Thunder then packed up his bag and said that the meat had to be burnt to ashes.

At this stage he invited the doctors present to look at his patient's leg. It was clear that the swelling had decreased and the colour had gone back to normal. The patient also said that he no longer felt any pain. Within a few minutes the patient, who had been bedridden for several weeks, was able to walk. He never suffered a recurrence of the problem.

Rolling Thunder's own explanation for his powers was that they came from the 'Great Spirit' – his name for what spiritual healers believe to be the beneficial healing energy of the universe.

Rev. William C. Brown

Spiritual healers are regarded rather differently in America from in Britain, where they can practise without restrictions. American healers have to be religious leaders as well, although there is nothing to stop them forming their own religions, as happened with Christian Science and Scientology. The Rev. William Brown, like George Chapman, performs spirit surgery while in trance. He is guided by doctors in the spirit world, of whom the most prominent are 'Dr Spaulding' and 'Dr Murphy'.

In his clinic William Brown always has a Bible open at Isaiah, chapter 30, verses 20 – 21, which he says is the only reference in the holy book to spirit teachers. These verses say:

'And though the Lord give you the bread of adversity, and the water of afflication, yet shall not thy teachers be removed into a corner any more, but thine eyes shall see thy teachers; And thine ears shall hear a word behind thee, saying, This is the way, walk ye in it, when ye turn to the right hand, and when ye turn to the left.'

When in a trance, William Brown speaks in the voices of his spirit guides, as George Chapman speaks in a voice supposedly that of Dr Lang. In one 'operation', witnessed by a spiritual healing researcher, David St Clair, author of the book *Psychic Healers,* the Rev. Brown 'injected' an imaginary hypodermic syringe into the neck of a patient who had been complaining about persistent pain since undergoing a surgical operation on his stomach.

St Clair was invited to feel the patient's pulse after the invisible hypodermic had been injected, and was surprised to feel that it was beating strongly. Soon, though, it became weaker and weaker. The Rev. Brown – or Dr Murphy – explained in an Irish accent that he had 'put enough material in him to calm him all the way down'. He informed the patient that there was a lot of scar tissue left from the earlier surgery.

After this, the Rev. Brown called on another spirit guide, 'Dr Thorndyke', and spoke now in an English accent. He made an incision with an invisible knife, clamped it open and 'operated'. After this, he stitched up the wound with an invisible needle and thread. After it was finished, the Rev. Brown asked his patient to get up. The patient felt very weak and looked white and drawn; he said he felt as if a rubber band had been stretched across his stomach.

Apart from that, the operation had been painless. Soon, the patient went into another room where he fell fast asleep. He reported later that the persistent pain had gone, and that there was no recurrence.

Henry Mandel

Mandel, from St. Petersburg, Florida, was a well-known healer who began his work at the age of sixty-three. Like all healers, he had his successes and failures. In one case, a forty-eight-year-old businessman who had developed lung cancer was told there was nothing more the doctors could do, and he did not have long to live. He decided to visit Henry Mandel, who gave him three healing sessions and then said that he was cured. A month later, the radiologist took X-rays and could not believe the results. He told the patient that he seemed to be cured as there was no trace of the cancer. Yet three months afterwards, the patient suddenly died.

In another case, a forty-five-year-old woman became partially paralysed, so that she had to give up her teaching job. She consulted several doctors and psychiatrists; they could find nothing wrong with her, yet she did not recover. Eventually, by now unable to walk, she sought out Henry Mandel. After only three treatments she was out of her wheelchair and walking as normal. But this patient, like the previous one, had a serious relapse three months later. She decided to visit Mandel again, and after treatment was walking once more.

These two examples of 'healing' illustrate that the treatment can be extremely temporary, as is often found by seriously ill people who visit the shrine of St Bernadette at Lourdes. Their condition seems to improve for a time, then goes back to what it was.

But Henry Mandel did have some lasting successes. A two-year-old Australian child, Christina, had something wrong with her right knee which caused her to limp. She soon found it extremely painful to walk, and her parents took her to leading orthopaedic surgeons. But by the age of two and a half Christina was in a permanent cast and had to take strong painkillers every night. Her eyesight began to be affected, probably because of the analgesics she was taking, and her parents decided to take her to Europe to see if a cure could be found.

When in Switzerland they stayed with Christina's grandmother, who had heard of Henry Mandel. Thinking they had nothing to lose, Christina's parents took the child to see him. After five of Mandel's treatments, Christina was completely better, and did not need to wear the cast or take painkillers again. She grew up perfectly normally.

HEALERS IN THE PHILIPPINES

One of the most mysterious phenomena of our times is the so-called 'psychic surgery' performed by a number of healers in the Philippines. These healers have been the subject of a great deal of investigation, and it is true to say that sleight-of-hand has often been discovered when the healers appear to be able to command blood and other tissue to come out of whole bodies. Some healers have also been discovered cheating when they apparently pack gauze and bandages into internal wounds without opening the skin.

But not all the Filipino healers have been fraudulent. Some undoubtedly have powers, although by now they have become so famous that many have started to cash in on the interest shown by the rest of the world.

Josefina Sison

One of the more famous female healers in the Philippines, Josefina Sison, is basically uneducated and lives with her husband and three children in a rural area of Luzon. She has been a professional healer since the age of eighteen.

One Australian patient reported that he had been in great pain from a cyst growing at the base of his spine. The condition, common among truck drivers, is chronic, and the only treatment is to remove the cyst surgically and pack the area with cotton wool. After fifteen years of suffering from this problem, he decided to visit Josefina in the Philippines. Since her house was four hours' drive from Manila he was in agony when he arrived. She asked him to lie face down on her wooden table, and within thirty seconds, according to the patient, removed a cyst about the size of a pigeon's egg. When he stood up there was no pain and no scar. The pain and the condition have not returned.

Josefina said in an interview that she can tell what is wrong with her patients through her 'third eye'. She has no medical knowledge at all. Sometimes, she said, her hands are guided by spirits to the area with the problem, and she hears a voice telling her what is wrong. Then, with other cases, she does automatic writing to find out what is the matter: the pencil writes out both the condition and the treatment.

British writer Allegra Taylor spent a year travelling to various parts of the world interviewing and investigating paranormal healers. She visited Josefina – who now has a proper healing centre, with chapel attached, and assistants – and describes the encounter in her book *I Fly Out with Bright Feathers*.

Everyone sat on wooden benches in the chapel, at the front of which was a raised portion with a green plastic-covered operating table on it, and a vase of dusty wax flowers. Behind Josephine's head was a sign stating: 'God does the work, I am only his instrument: please pray.' Another gave directives to be adhered to after receiving healing: 'Do not eat meat or anything sour or cold. Do not smoke or drink alcohol. Do not take a bath or shower (sponge with lukewarm water). Rest. Do not exert strenuous effort. Refrain from romance. Eat vegetables, salad and fresh fruit. Pray and relax. Be at Peace.' . . .

All the operations are performed with lightning speed in full view of everyone, except in a few cases where the nature of the complaint is very personal; then a cursory curtain is whipped across . . .

From my seat in the front row I still couldn't really see closely enough, so I asked if I could stand behind the table. Josephine, wearing a short-sleeved dress, with only a large bucket of water for washing her hands and a waste bin for chucking the gore into, began her operations. She gave most cases a quick rummage and pulled out clots, but every once in a while she would pull at great wads of what looked like leaf compost or coconut matting and, on one occasion, a length of bloody cloth.

Another extraordinary sight is her famous cotton-wool routine. She breaks off small wads from a normal commercial roll, soaks them in consecrated coconut oil and appears to dematerialise them right through the skin. Sometimes, as in the case of a little girl with a chest complaint, she leaves them inside the body to be removed another day and sometimes, as in the case of a man with a brain tumour, she stuffs it in one ear and pulls it, streaked with blood, out of the other. The cotton wool is believed to 'suck up' the disease.

After observing these operations, Allegra Taylor felt that sleight-of-hand had to be ruled out, and that Josefina did demonstrate remarkable powers. But, she says, most people who have come to watch have pronounced it all so much fraud and trickery. The success rate for Filipino healers is usually put at about 30 per cent, which may not sound all that high – but most patients who make their way to these unorthodox healers have been pronounced incurable by the medical profession.

Tony Agpaoa

Agpaoa, who died in 1984 from a brain haemorrhage, was probably the most famous Filipino healer of all. He received very little formal education and began working as a healer at the age of twelve. Towards the end of his life, when he became very rich and famous, he was seeing patients from all over the world at his clinic in Baguio City.

There seems little doubt that at the height of his powers he could be a very remarkable healer, but from all accounts he became very greedy, charging potential patients $1000 in advance for healing. As his fees increased, so his powers waned, according to reports.

But many of his more dramatic successes have been well documented. One concerns a woman in her thirties who was dying from cancer. The disease had progressed so far that doctors had given her six months to live. She could no longer do anything and was permanently hospitalized, being fed intravenously. As the medical profession could do no more, it was suggested that she make the journey to see Tony; her husband and doctors felt that, although she might well die *en route*, she had nothing to lose. After being seen by Tony she was given a series of eight psychic operations. She remained in the

Philippines for five weeks, during which time she was able to walk and eat again normally. The cancer, which had spread to her lungs, cleared up completely and she made a complete recovery.

During his lifetime Tony, in common with many other Filipino healers, was extensively studied and observed by Western doctors and scientists. Dr Sigrun Seutemann, a German medical practitioner who has observed literally thousands of medical treatments being performed by Tony, reported that she noticed definite changes in Tony's behaviour and demeanour while the healing was in progress.

> *He radiates energy from his body to the patient. The energy he exchanges with the patient depends on the body of the patient − i.e., if the patient is not receptive, the energy exchange is low. . . . The main problem with Tony is attuning with Europeans. The Europeans are not so receptive because of their intellectual hang-ups. Tony can treat a hundred Filipinos a day without any difficulty, whereas only fifty Europeans require much greater effort.*
>
> *If a patient is anxious or fearful on arrival, this affects the physical and energy body. Tony aims to remove blockages in the system, and rebalance and correct the flow of energy to the organs. When balanced, the patient feels much better.*

Arigo

José Pedro de Freitas, known as Arigo, who died in 1971 at the age of forty-nine, was a Brazilian healer who in his lifetime became world-famous. According to researcher Andrija Puharich, who made several films of Arigo's work, this healer never charged anybody, and to support himself was at various times a miner, an agricultural labourer and a clerical assistant in an office. Like George Chapman and Leah Doctors, he claimed to be channelling a long-dead doctor who worked through him to perform miraculous psychic operations. According to a story in *Time* magazine in 1972, Arigo saw up to three hundred patients a day, and treated every ailment known. Most of his patients, the report goes on to say, were healed.

Basically uneducated, like many South American healers, Arigo could apparently look at a patient and diagnose within minutes what was wrong, and with astonishing accuracy. He could even tell, without measuring, what the blood pressure of certain patients was.

Arigo also prescribed medicines for his patients, often when these had no apparent connection with the illness being treated. Keen on vitamins, he was one of the first healers to prescribe megadoses, now a common form of therapy among certain American doctors. He could also, according to observers, perform actual operations – as opposed to spirit operations – without anaesthesia, yet the patient would feel no pain. Very often, according to reports, the knives or scissors he used were not sterilized. Yet post-operative infections never developed.

Arigo claimed that he channelled a physician whom he identified as 'Dr Fritz', and performed diagnoses and operations only on instruction from this doctor, now in the spirit world. Arigo's work has been documented on film, and closely investigated. During his lifetime, the many observers who came to his clinic – a simple wooden building – were able to testify that he really did perform miraculous operations and diagnoses and offer uncannily accurate treatment.

Like most other spiritual healers, Arigo specialized in conditions that doctors were unable to cure or treat. He was very successful with all forms of cancer, and prescribed many drugs to shrink tumours. He refused to treat patients who, in his opinion, would get just as good treatment from their own orthodox doctors.

Many healers, many different methods. Sometimes their healing results in a complete recovery; at other times there may be only a temporary improvement, or none at all. Because unorthodox healing has become such a world-wide phenomenon, and it is impossible to ignore the fact that many remarkable results have been achieved, it is not surprising that their work has been closely investigated by scientists, doctors and psychical researchers.

With the Filipino healers, researchers have been mainly concerned to see whether they can expose fraudulent practices, simply because what they do or appear to do – pull lengths of bloody cloth out of patients without opening up the body, extract visible tumours without the use of knives or other surgical methods, pack cotton wool inside patients' bodies apparently by magic – seems so completely impossible. If the Filipinos can practise psychic surgery, and take away tumours without surgical instruments or anaesthetics, why can't ordinary doctors do it? After all, it would save an enormous amount of pain, suffering, hospital time and money.

The practice of psychic surgery, where actual tumours or material objects are apparently passed through living flesh without leaving scars or wounds, seems confined to the Philippines. Healers in Britain and America who have practised psychic surgery do so using spirit guides and invisible instruments. Here the question of sleight-of-hand is inappropriate, and researchers have concentrated on trying to understand the powers that certain spiritual healers seem to have. They do undoubtedly have remarkable successes, even though no healer will ever guarantee complete recovery – or even any kind of recovery.

3 ❧ *The Scientific Rationale*

There have been so many instances of seriously ill people being cured by spiritual healers that it is impossible to dismiss it all as complete rubbish. Whatever the sceptics say – that the healing was due to the power of suggestion, to the strength of the placebo effect, to the strong personality or charisma of the healer – there is no doubt at all that apparently miraculous healings have taken place.

Over the past twenty or so years a number of scientists, intrigued by reports of the success of spiritual healing, have decided to try and investigate the mystery under proper laboratory conditions. If healing without medicine or surgery is a fact, then clearly something has to happen. But what?

Experiments with mice in Canada
The first serious scientific investigator of modern times has been Dr Bernard Grad, of McGill University, Canada, who felt that it must be possible for 'paranormal' healings to be tested in the laboratory. If something definitely happened, then it should be possible to show this by modern scientific means. Dr Grad wanted to try and find a definitive answer to this question: does the 'laying on of hands' method of healing cure people simply by the power of suggestion (whatever that might be), or is there another force at work, some kind of energy which could actually be measured in the laboratory?

Because human beings are notoriously susceptible to the power of suggestion, Dr Grad chose mice for his initial experiments. He asked a well-known healer, Colonel Oskar Estebany, who had discovered in himself healing abilities when doctors and medical care were short during the Hungarian Revolution of 1956, if he would cooperate with him. Estebany agreed, and the experiment was set up.

Dr Grad 'softened up' the laboratory mice by stroking and handling them before the experiment started, then under anaesthetic removed a piece of skin from their backs. After this was done, he weighed all forty-eight mice and measured their wounds: all the wounds were as similar as possible in size, shape and severity.

Dr Grad divided the mice up into three groups. One group was to be treated by Colonel Estebany by moving his hands across the mice's backs; the second group were left to recover on their own; while the third group were to be subjected to heat treatment of the same temperature as that produced by the healer's hands hovering above them.

The skin wounds were carefully measured and monitored. It was found that the mice treated by Estebany healed up quickly, but that there was no difference between the untreated and the heat-treated groups.

This experiment was repeated at the University of Manitoba under strict conditions, using a far larger sample of three hundred mice. In this experiment, one group of mice were treated by people who did not claim to possess any healing ability. The results were exactly the same as those produced by the original experiment. The healer-treated mice recovered quickly, but those treated by non-healers did not do so well. In fact, mice treated by medical students healed more slowly than those left on their own.

These two experiments seemed to show that something beyond the power of suggestion was at work, as mice are clearly not amenable to suggestion.

Experiments with growing barley seeds

Dr Grad then decided to try a different type of experiment, this time with barley seeds. Some seeds were placed in a saline solution 'treated' by healers, while others were placed in an identical solution not so treated. Elaborate equipment was used which could detect growth at the rate of a thousandth of an inch.

It was found that the 'treated' plants started to grow far more quickly than the untreated ones.

The results of these experiments seemed to show that something – some other kind of reality, perhaps – was at work. Invisible yet potent forces appeared to be emanating from those who appeared to possess healing ability.

Dr Grad then felt that people's state of mind might affect the outcome of disease, and also their 'green finger' ability. He believed that mentally disturbed patients might actually hinder the healing process, and set out to try and show this. Three people – a depressive woman aged twenty-six, a man of the same age diagnosed as psychotic, and a gardener with noted green fingers were asked to hold a jar containing barley seeds. Here, it was found that they grew far quicker when 'treated' by the healer. But the seeds 'treated' by the psychotic man started to grow *much more slowly* than those held by mentally sound people used as 'controls'. It was also found that the seeds held by the depressed woman grew relatively quickly. The reason for this, postulated Dr Grad, was that when she was told about the experiment her mood changed, and she 'cradled the bottle like an infant', according to reports.

The conclusion Dr Grad reached from his experiments was that some energy was at work which could make a difference to humans, animals and even plants. He concluded that the 'green finger' ability is akin to the mysterious powers possessed by spiritual healers.

Demonstrating 'healing energy'

In 1967 a Dr Robert W. Miller of Atlanta, Georgia, undertook another experiment with seeds. He chose rye grass for its quick-growing abilities, and worked with two well-known American healers, Olga and Ambrose Worrall, a husband and wife team. Dr Miller decided to test the strength of 'absent healing' and asked the Worralls to hold the seedlings in their prayers at a distance of six hundred miles. Dr Miller found that at 9 p.m. precisely, when the Worralls were to begin praying for the seeds, they began to grow. The laboratory door was closed and all other possible inducements to growing removed from the room, and the seeds' growth was then measured on highly sensitive instruments. The Worralls later told Dr Miller that they had visualized the rye grass filled with light and energy. Apparently, it had responded.

Not content with this, Dr Miller wanted to show that 'healing energy' is an absolute reality, not simply an airy-fairy idea. If it exists, he stated, then surely it must be possible to show it in some way, given present-day highly sensitive recording instruments. He felt that a cloud chamber, such as those used by physicists to show up high-energy nuclear particles, might also be able to indicate the presence of 'healing energy'. Cloud chambers consist of a glass vessel with an aluminium floor. The chamber floor is covered with a thin layer of methyl alcohol and the chamber is put on a block of dry ice. When a charged particle is passed through, there is a misty condensation which can be clearly seen.

Olga Worrall placed her hands on the side of the cloud chamber, and 'treated' the contents as if they were a patient, sending out healing energy. It was noticed that a distinct wave pattern developed in the mist, exactly the same as that made when her hands moved over the chamber sides. Dr Miller also succeeded in producing wave patterns inside the chamber when other practising healers were used. Dr Miller then asked Mrs Worrall to give the cloud chamber 'absent healing', which she did from her home six hundred miles away. Distinct waves were again produced. But members of the research team were unable to make any impression on the mist, however hard they tried. Dr Miller also discovered, in more experiments, that solutions of copper chloride turned blue when treated by Mrs Worrall, but remained green when treated by non-healers. He also discovered that the surface tension of water is reduced when receiving energy from a healer's hands.

Dr Miller decided that healing energy must be similar to magnetic energy. When treated by a magnet, both the surface tension of water was reduced, and the copper chloride crystals also turned blue. Powerful magnets, too, could make rye grass grow quickly.

According to the book *Healers and the Healing Process*, the experiments undertaken by Dr Grad and Dr Miller show that:

1. An energy associated with healing does exist, and it can be measured with suitable instruments.

2. Water which has been treated by a healer or a magnet changes the colour of a crystal solution, and thus gives visual indication of the presence of the healing energy.

3. Water treated by a healer or a magnet changes surface tension, hydrogen bonding and the electrical properties of water.

4. A healer is most effective when in an alpha relaxed state of consciousness.

The 'alpha state' refers to the frequency of brainwaves, which can be measured on an electroencephalograph (EEG). The normal waking state is beta, followed by alpha which is the 'meditation' brainwave, then delta and theta, which are sleeping states. We now know that creativity happens most often in the alpha state; also that, for many people, it takes practice to get into this state and to slow down the brainwaves when waking.

Ambrose Worrall believed that the energy coming from a healer's hands was very similar to electrical energy, as its action was almost identical. It flows, he said, from a high-potential source (God, the cosmos) to a person or object at lower potential.

The Society for Psychical Research in both Britain and America has undertaken research into 'healing energies' to see whether there is anything there, other than in the mind of the recipient. The Society was founded in 1882 by a group of Cambridge scholars who, concerned that materialism seemed to be gaining ground, wanted to see whether scientific evidence could be provided for survival after death. Since then, the Society has conducted numerous research projects into all kinds of paranormal phenomena, ghosts, out-of-the-body experiences and the evidence or otherwise for the presence of healing energies.

One researcher, Douglas Dean of Princeton University, undertook some experiments in 1982 to try and show whether healers could alter the molecular structure of water. He asked a number of them to put their hands round a flask of water and send out 'healing'. Dr Dean found that there was an alteration in molecular structure, and came to the conclusion that healers could definitely affect molecules, but his experiments have not so far been written up in a scientific journal.

Dr Dolores Kreiger, Professor of Nursing at New York Hospital, also decided to try a healing experiment. Fascinated by the work of Dr Bernard Grad, she asked Colonel Estebany to see if he could alter the basic structure of haemoglobin, the red blood corpuscles. She was amazed that his 'laying on of hands' actually affected the red blood cells for the better: they were healthier after Estebany's 'healing'.

Maxwell Cade's researches

The other main scientific researcher into spiritual healing has been C. Maxwell Cade, mentioned in Chapter 2. Cade, who died in 1975, studied medicine and clinical psychology at London University. During the Second World War he joined the Royal Navy, and subsequently worked for the Royal Naval Scientific Service carrying out research into radiation physics. At the same time he was personally interested in Zen Buddhism, and learned many relaxation techniques. He became interested in psychical research, and from 1973 to 1975 was honorary secretary of the Society.

In 1960 Cade became interested in studying altered states of consciousness from a scientific point of view, and pioneered much research into biofeedback techniques, with the idea of combining ancient wisdom with current technology. His book *The Awakened Mind,* co-written with novelist and New Age pioneer Nona Coxhead Bell, describes some of his research with spiritual healers into brainwave patterns, which could be accurately measured on an EEG machine. The machine provides constant feedback to internal states, as it monitors the rhythms of electrical activity which originate in the brain. This can be combined with a simple skin resistance meter which can be strapped on to the hand and shows through skin temperature changes how agitated or relaxed people are. In his search for objective evidence of 'healing rhythms', Cade also invented a machine he called the Mind Mirror – a small black box about the size of an answerphone – which shows up in a series of red dots all the major brainwave patterns. Electrodes are strapped to the subject's head and the machine starts recording instantly.

Cade carried out many experiments with healers Rose

Gladden and Addie Raeburn. He noticed that within fifteen minutes of starting healing, their skin resistance had increased by 150 per cent. This indicated that they were already in a highly relaxed, non-aroused state. Cade also noticed that, when both healer and patient were wired up to an EEG machine, the patients quickly began to develop the same brainwave patterns as the healer. In both cases, the frequencies became slower and the patterns indicated greater relaxation. Cade believed that for healing to take place, there has to be a definite relaxation response which can be shown up on the machines. On Cade's machine, the brainwaves of both healers and patients returned to their normal, non-healing state after the session was complete.

In one case that Cade investigated, Addie Raeburn was carrying out healing on a patient who had received very extensive leg injuries from a bomb accident. The machine revealed that, as her hands moved over the patient's injuries, his brainwave patterns were altered so that relaxation took place and arousal and anxiety were diminished. Healers, believed Cade, have the ability to 'dissolve the wall' between themselves and other people, and are able to bring about harmony where before there was disharmony. Effective healers, he was able to show, always have an enormous empathy with their patients and an ability to still their minds, to make them become calm and undisturbed. In addition, the very best healers can extinguish their personal egos and become part of something they feel is 'higher than themselves'.

Cade felt that it was impossible to state in truly scientific terms what healers actually do. Although it is absolutely without question that they are able to change brainwave patterns for the better in their subjects, nobody knows how they can do this. Healers who are extremely psychic – as most healers must be – have brainwave patterns which are very different from, say, a bank manager's. On the Mind Mirror, healers' brainwaves indicate that they have continual cross-traffic between the conscious and the unconscious. In this, they are the complete opposite from, say, psychopathic criminals who seem to be able to allow nothing from their conscious mind to get into their unconscious; their alpha waves, which normally form the bridge between the conscious and the unconscious mind, are tightly shut and allow no through traffic. This is why they can perform terrible crimes and appear to feel no remorse. People who appear unable to empathize with others would also not be good healers.

Effective healers are, above all, people who seem able to reach out to others, to know what they are thinking or feeling, and who feel positive enough themselves to help bring about an effective change. It seems likely that there is some energy exchange between healers and patients, but Maxwell Cade was never able to get to the bottom of the source of this energy. Does it come from the healer, from God, from some cosmic force – or what? Nobody yet has the answer, but Cade was certainly able to show that 'something' was happening – and that healers are able to induce a definite beneficial response in their patients.

In his book, Cade states that he is happy to say that a healing response has occurred if the healer can, in a single session, produce a noticeable alleviation of pain and discomfort in the patient's condition which is sustained for a substantial length of time. On the machines, he looked for evidence of normalization of the activity of the sympathetic nervous system.

Cade observed that a patient will always be more relaxed after a successful healing session. The skin resistance meter gives accurate readings on levels of arousal before and after a healing session. The physiological changes which come about appear to be the result of the ability of the healer to induce some kind of deep relaxation in the patient.

Cade's Mind Mirror does not just show up brainwave patterns: it also indicates what is going on in both the left and right hemispheres of the brain. We now know that the right hemisphere deals mainly with intuition – what may be called psychic awareness and creativity – while the left hemisphere is associated with logical, rational thinking and judgment. In healthy people, Cade observed, there will always be symmetry of brain function on both sides. Where the right and left brain patterns are uncoordinated and out of harmony, there is likely to be some kind of dysfunction. This may manifest itself as mental or physical illness, or both. Healers, Cade noticed, always have exceptionally symmetrical brainwave patterns. Also, when healing, they concentrate very hard on what they are doing, and do not allow their minds to wander.

The key is relaxation

The phenomenon of absent healing was also investigated by Cade. He carried out experiments with healer Edgar Chase, putting Chase in one room and the patient in another. Both were wired up – quite painlessly – to the Mind Mirror. As the clock struck four, Edgar Chase was to commence 'absent healing' for the benefit of the patient in the other room. As soon as healing started, Chase's brainwave patterns altered and he went into the 'higher state' of consciousness. Fifteen seconds later, the patient's brainwave patterns began to alter, to read similarly to Chases's.

Before setting up in practice as a healer, Edgar Chase was a physicist. He said that he was always aware of severe tension in seriously ill patients, and that it was their tension, as much as anything, that kept them ill. In the early 1970s Chase started using a skin resistance meter to see what happened when healing was being given. In a report sent to Cade, Chase remarked that, during healing, nervous tension in patients was reduced by between 40 and 80 per cent. Once again the importance of relaxation was stressed. Chase felt that it was only once relaxation had been induced, that real healing could begin. He wrote: 'The response of the patient to direct treatment of his problem is accelerated significantly when he is completely relaxed. Migraine can disappear in five minutes as opposed to an hour ... an asthmatic attack disappears completely in twenty minutes. The instrument records all changes and is a valid key to the monitoring of progress ....'

The advantage of the Mind Mirror and the skin resistance meters – which are very small and can be used by the patients themselves – is that people can actually see that something is happening. As relaxation is induced, the needle swings round to show a calm and steady response.

Cade concluded that, in order for healers to be effective, their own mental and physical health must be good. Otherwise, their own brain patterns will be out of harmony. Mental depression, he said, can deprive healers of their power; they must be rock-steady and able to stay calm through all vicissitudes. To some extent this is an ability which can be learnt, and the development of biofeedback machines has enabled people to become more relaxed, as they can monitor their response and

progress. After all, you can't argue with a machine. Cade
hypothesized that around fifteen out of every hundred people
had the potential ability to be healers of others; the rest did not
have the psychic, opened state necessary for the healing power
to be operational. But, said Cade, most of us could increase our
healing potential. We may have faulty technique, we may not
be preparing ourselves well enough, or we may allow our
subjective feelings to take over. We also may not concentrate
hard enough when trying out healing. Cade's machines
established that total concentration is necessary to channel the
healing power effectively.

All unusual abilities in people, Cade stated, could be shown
up clearly on the Mind Mirror. The symmetrical brain patterns
were noticed in healers, yogis and swamis and also those at the
very top of their profession. Such states as self-esteem, self-
confidence and serenity, a belief in oneself, all can be indicated
on the Mind Mirror and the skin resistance meters. Anxiety and
fear are very common – and a standard block to wellness.

Since Maxwell Cade's time, it has been established that the
relaxation response can have a definite beneficial effect on the
immune system. Cade's work is now being carried on and developed by his widow Isabel and his colleague Geoffrey Blundell.

Maxwell Cade's work is continued today
I paid a visit to their offices in Shepherds Bush in West London.
Geoffrey Blundell looks like a typical scientist, with grey beard
and sandals, and he tends to cycle round central London. Like
Cade, Blundell is interested in Tibetan mysticism and has paid
many visits to Tibet. He said he just loves to invent, and his office
is a 'mad scientist's' paradise of hundreds of little machines,
wires and complicated circuits.

Blundell feels that his work with sensitive brainwave and skin
resistance machines has proved that, in order for healing to take
place, brain rhythms have to slow down and there must be
relaxation of mind and body. 'So many people imagine that
relaxation means the same as flaking out in front of the
television' he said.

*Our machines show that relaxation actually takes hard work and
practice. In order for healing to have any long-term effect, there must*

be deep relaxation on the part of the patient. It's so easy to have an intellectual idea that you are relaxing, but our machines will very often tell you differently. The development of our machines shows people that all physiological changes can actually be measured.

Healing happens when there is transfer of some kind of mental energy from the healer to the patient. I don't know where this comes from, but the Mind Mirror can show when people have been healed. A few years ago a woman with serious cancer was shown to have been healed by her vicar, who also had healing ability. When a cancer specialist, Dr Alex Forbes, looked at the rhythms, he said that there was medically no way this patient could have been healed without her whole system being poisoned. Yet at her next test, the Mind Mirror's analysis was shown to be accurate – there was no cancer present any more. Unless there is harmony between healer and patient, nothing can happen.

Healers must themselves go into an altered state of consciousness in order to perform healing. We know that the alpha rhythm is the bridge to creativity, and that healing is an aspect of creativity. But also the alpha state can be pathological. There has to be harmony in the other states as well. We call alpha the neutral gear – in itself it does nothing, but you can't drive a car unless you also have neutral.

In order for healing to be permanent, the patient must recognize that something is happening. Otherwise, the effect will be extremely temporary. But we have shown on our machines that spiritual healing is not at all 'faith' healing. Bruce McManaway was able to heal animals using exactly the same techniques as he used on humans. Both animals and plants will respond to a healer.

Healing is really waking up dormant energy. But without seeing it for themselves on the machines, people may have a hard job to believe it. We can now measure the response, if any, towards particular healers. It goes from sluggishness towards activity. We all have higher states of consciousness, but many people cannot access them. We have shown that healers have this access, and that they can enable their patients to be aware of them as well.

Spiritual healers and the medical profession

A recent development in Britain is that a growing number of doctors are referring some of their patients to spiritual healers, or are working with these healers in the surgery. GPs who work together with healers say that patients like them, and that there is a very useful outcome – a far lower prescription rate for those patients who have had healing. One GP, who refused to be named for professional reasons, said that he realized recently that he too was a healer: 'I am so scared about revealing this to my colleagues as I do not want to be labelled a crazy man. But two and a half years ago I experienced a blinding blue light and realized I was a healer. There was the feeling of tremendous energy. It was very exciting.'

This doctor says that he works on an 'intuitive level' and gets a sense of where the trouble is. He finds he does not have to prescribe so much now, as patients 'find their own healing from inside'. He did add, though, that some patients have left his list because they worry that he might be able to read their minds.

A recent survey of 140 GPs in the Avon district showed that 17 per cent have had positive dealings with spiritual healers. And Sussex GP Dr Craig Brown now lets healer Del Ralph sit in on his surgery sessions. Before beginning the session, both doctor and healer meditate for a few minutes to clarify their minds and let the healing energies in. Dr Brown says that there have so far been no miracle cures – nobody has recovered from terminal cancer, for instance. But patients gain tranquillity from the healing session. Dr Brown also points out that not all patients are happy with spiritual healing. Some believe it is connected with spiritualism, the occult or faith healing.

Dr Dermot Kelleher, another Sussex GP, has a spiritual healer running his own clinic from the surgery itself, and is convinced that healing has a place in general practice. Dr Kelleher has found healing particularly beneficial for cases of severe back pain, and his prescribing costs are now 25 per cent lower than the national average. He has hardly ever prescribed tranquillizers or mind-altering drugs since the healer took up residence.

Dr Michael Massey, a south London GP, regularly refers patients to a spiritual healing centre in Kent and says that he now never prescribes tranquillizers. To date, around 120 medical studies have been carried out on healers, and of these, sixty-seven have demonstrated that healing has a definite positive effect.

The Confederation of Healing Organizations in Britain has worked out a code of conduct with the Royal Colleges and the

General Medical Council. It has also begun a series of clinical trials designed to prove scientifically that spiritual healing can help patients with such complaints as arthritis, ulcers, cancer and diabetes, and in pain control. The Campaign against Health Fraud, also known as Quackbusters, is in favour of spiritual healing. Their medical spokesman, Dr Vaughan Smith, feels that such healing is perfectly permissible when combined with orthodox medical treatment. Dr Smith says that spiritual healers do not charge exorbitant fees, and are 'less of a problem' than other alternative practitioners.

Quackery and fraud are also discouraged by the stringent regulations that must be followed by healers. The position in Britain at the moment is that anybody who wishes to set up as a professional healer must be sponsored by two other qualified healers and also provide names of four successful cases. The healer must also agree to abide by the Confederation's code of conduct, and agree not to try and supplant the doctor.

Clearly, more scientific work is needed before we know exactly what the 'healing energy' is and how exactly it may be transferred from healer to patient. We also need to know how the healer manages to access so much spare healing energy, when the ill person, who needs it more, can't seem to utilize it. But the work that has been done so far definitely establishes that energies are transferred, and that spiritual healing can make a difference for the better.

Matthew Manning – the subject of extensive research

Still only in his early thirties, Matthew Manning has been called the 'most extensively tested healer in Britain'. He is also one of the most popular. He now concentrates almost entirely on helping cancer patients in conjunction with their standard medical treatment, and at the time of writing has a nine-month waiting list. Matthew sees fifty-two patients a week at the Matthew Manning Centre at Bury St Edmunds in Suffolk, and is in great demand all over the world for his healing skills.

The eldest of three children, Matthew was born into a comfortable middle-class family in Cambridge; his father, Derek, was an architect. At the age of eleven, strange poltergeist-like occurrences began to centre round him, both at home and at boarding school. Beds began to levitate, pools of water appeared from nowhere, hot spots were noticed on walls and objects flew around. This must have been great fun for the boys at Matthew's school, but the headmaster was not amused and wanted him to leave. At first he thought that Matthew was playing tricks, but later he became convinced that the paranormal phenomena which seemed to centre round him were completely genuine.

In 1971 Matthew managed to put a stop to the poltergeist activity by developing an ability for automatic writing. He would hear spirit voices supposedly from the Cambridgeshire Webbe family (members of which were long deceased) and write down what they said, in handwriting completely different from his own. He later tried automatic drawing, and produced several works of art in the styles of Picasso, Matisse, Durer and Aubrey Beardsley; in normal consciousness Matthew had very limited artistic talent. It was after demonstrating his apparent ability to alter the structure of cancer cells that Manning set up as a full-time healer, at the age of twenty-two. He has never had any other job.

Between 1977 and 1982 a large number of scientific experiments were carried out on Matthew, to try and establish whether he really did have some kind of psychic or paranormal ability, and whether he could influence living and non-living objects. A month-long series of experiments in California with established scientists – not parapsychologists – discovered that Manning did appear to possess genuinely paranormal abilities, that he was not a fraud or a trickster, and that he could without doubt influence living cells.

The first odd thing that the researchers discovered was that strange things happened whenever Manning was in the vicinity. Before any experiments were set up, weird high-frequency sounds were heard, lifts mysteriously jammed, and a long-unwound wall clock suddenly started ticking. Keys belonging to one researcher were found bent, and windscreen wipers stopped working of their own accord. A tape recorder began to malfunction during a talk with Matthew, but resumed its normal functioning soon afterwards. Engineers could find nothing wrong with it when it was taken in for repair. A colour tape in a TV studio played in black and white when it should have been in colour.

None of these happenings necessarily has anything to do with healing, of course, but they suggested to the researchers that Matthew did possess unusual abilities. In one experiment, carried out by Professor F.W. Lorenz of the Department of Animal Physiology at the University of California, involving an EEG machine, it was shown that brainwaves became synchronized between Matthew and a number of subjects.

Another experiment, conducted by Dr James L. Hickman of the Washington Research Centre in San Francisco, attempted to discover whether Matthew could influence the rate at which plants grew. Three small glass vials were filled up with commercial rye grass seeds and sealed. Dr Hickman gave one of the vials to Matthew and asked him to try and increase the normal yield. Matthew held the vial between his hands, closed his eyes, concentrated for five minutes and then gave the vial back to Dr Hickman. A second vial was given to Matthew with instructions to *decrease* the normal yield. Matthew did the same thing, and then returned the vial to Dr Hickman. He had no contact at all with the third vial. The seeds were then locked away by a colleague of Dr Hickman's.

They were later transferred to soil, and each group of carefully labelled seeds were kept in identical conditions. Dr Hickman measured the seeds nine, ten and eleven days after planting. He noticed that there was a significant increase in the ones Matthew had been asked to influence positively. There was no difference, however, in the growth of the seeds which Matthew had been instructed to influence negatively: their growth rate was identical to that of the untreated seeds. A further experiment with radish seeds showed that the 'treated' seeds showed more green growth than the untreated ones, although there was no difference in the taste.

More experiments were tried by various American researchers. During 1977 and 1978 Matthew visited the Mind Science Foundation in San Antonio, where laboratory situations were set up which attempted to show whether he could influence living creatures and cells. The conclusion the researchers came to was that Matthew definitely had the ability to influence 'living target systems', as they were called.

In the first experiment, he was asked to try and influence the movements of a gerbil on an activity wheel in the next room.

The gerbil had been denied access to its activity wheel for some time before the experiment. Matthew imagined the gerbil running quickly round the wheel, and at the time that he was visualizing this happening, the gerbil's activity increased. All the movements were carefully measured on sensitive instruments.

For the second of this batch of experiments Matthew was asked to influence the movements of a knife fish, which sends out electrical signals. Here again Matthew was in another room, and imagined the fish swimming in a particular direction. As he did so, the fish obliged. Again, everything was wired up so that the amount of movement in the right direction could be carefully recorded, and there was no room for error.

So far, so good. For the third experiment at the Foundation, Matthew was asked to try and influence the behaviour of human living organisms. For this, a human volunteer was introduced to Matthew, and told that the young healer would try to influence his autonomic (not under conscious control) nervous system activity. The volunteer sat in a chair with the first and third fingers of his left hand attached to electrodes with Velcro. He was told nothing about the timing of the experiment, or when Manning would start to try and influence his nervous system. Matthew was shown a pack of cards with different instructions on them, and when the one saying 'Influence' came up, Matthew got to work.

His task was to try and influence the volunteer to emit a greater frequency of galvanic skin responses – in other words, to appear more het up. For this, Matthew imagined the volunteer becoming emotionally more activated, and he also imagined the polygraph pen – which was recording the increased activity, if any – making large deflections. Twenty trials were held in all, and after taking careful measurements it was decided that Matthew was able to activate the nervous system of the volunteer by mental effort and at a distance.

For the next experiment, Matthew as asked to try to halt the destruction rate of human whole blood cells in a glass jar as they were being subjected to degenerative stress. He had already shown a considerable ability in another experiment to exert influence on laboratory-cultured cancer cells. By sending out 'healing' to these cells by the laying on of hands technique, he had been able to alter their structure in the direction of 'health'. Strong similar effects had also been noted when Matthew tried to influence these same cancer cells at a distance.

In the new blood trials, Matthew placed his hands above the tube of cells and attempted to decrease the rate of destruction: he visualized strong white light round the cells and imagined them as intact and resistant to the saline solution that was threatening to destroy them. He also attempted to influence them at a distance. It was found that Matthew was able to halt the destruction of the cells considerably when he attempted to influence them; the cells which were not 'influenced' destructed at the normal, expected rate.

The conclusion from this series of experiments was that Matthew was definitely able to exert an above-chance influence on a 'variety of biological systems'. But interestingly, the researchers found that people without any special claimed psychic powers could also influence living material when they tried. Perhaps this means we all have some of the healer in us?

The researchers felt that biological systems, which are always changing, growing or dying anyway, are very likely to be subject to the influence of 'psychic healing'. Some further experiments with Matthew in England, involving guessing what poetry and drawings were contained in sealed envelopes, and others using pendulums, revealed no special powers. But a large-scale experiment conducted with Professor Arthur Ellison of the City University in London showed that Matthew did appear able to exert his influence on infra-red machines. The experiments in Britain were carried out under the auspices of the Society for Psychical Research, who are always notoriously unwilling to accept anything as truly paranormal until it has been through several controlled trials under laboratory conditions. But Professor Ellison and his colleagues concluded that Matthew was able to exert an influence on infra-red machines that did seem to be paranormal. At least, there appeared to be no other explanation for what happened to the machines.

It is probably because of Matthew's great success with 'healing' cancer cells under laboratory conditions that he has decided to specialize in treating cancer patients. Also, he says, these are usually the most ill and the most desperate of people. He hasn't got time, he maintains, to treat those people who aren't really ill, when thousands of dying people are contacting him every day.

In the *Proceedings of the Society for Psychical Research* for 1982, where the British experiments are written up, Matthew wrote an afterword. He says there that, in order for him to be able to influence living (or even non-living) matter, three conditions have to be present. These are:

1. He has to have a strong desire for the event to occur;
2. He has to believe it is possible;
3. He must believe it can reasonably take place.

If there is no belief, his whole mind, he says, works against it and no results are achieved. He also says that there must be at least some rapport between him and the researcher. If this is replaced by a sceptical, closed-mind attitude the experiment is not likely to be a success.

As a healer, he says that the mental attitudes needed to encourage the healing response take practice and experience to attain. 'Thoughts are energy and energy influences that which is material,' he has said. 'You create your own reality. It's that simple!'

Matthew says that in order to have a positive influence on living cells, he has to calm himself and expel all unnecessary thoughts from his mind. He has to reach a state of blankness before any healing can take place. Then his imagination gets to work. He first of all imagines himself expanding his consciousness like ripples in a stream. The images become ever more complicated until eventually he is on top of a mountain and has a sense of peace and strength. At this stage, he senses warmth coming into his hands and going into the cells. He visualizes the cells being surrounded by powerful white light, and then he talks to them. If blood cells are under stress, he assures them that light and energy will protect them.

If he is trying to influence cancer cells, he tells them that their useful purpose is over and their level of reality has ended. He never tells cancer cells to die, he says: he always proceeds by positive, gentle thinking. 'I never wish that anything should die' he has stated.

Matthew Manning's belief about healing now is that he only does what patients could, in the right state of consciousness, do for themselves. The trouble is that when they are desperately ill, they are very often unable to get into the required condition of calmness and peace to bring about the healing response.

The indefatigable paranormal researcher, Brian Inglis, summed up the British experiments with Manning by saying that there is very possibly a paranormal ability at work. If Manning is able to exert a therapeutic effect on diseased cells, this happens very probably because the cells are paranormally shaken out of their diseased condition, and then encouraged to become healthy by having soothing and positive images suggested to them, Inglis hypothesizes. He suggests that paranormal healing, if indeed there is such a thing, is such a two-step process.

Inglis and other psychical researchers feel that far more experiments are needed before we can be absolutely certain that there is a truly paranormal effect, something operating outside known scientific laws, at work. He says that if other healers were as willing as Matthew Manning to subject themselves to experiments conducted under proper laboratory conditions, and have the results tape-recorded and properly written up, 'we might get somewhere'.

Further research and investigations into the different methods of healing are described in Chapter 4.

PART II

4 ❧ Types of Healing

Although spiritual healing can be basically defined as a transfer of some kind of energy from the healer to the patient, there are very many different types of such healing. Since about 1955, when the National Federation of Spiritual Healing was formed, all types of non-medical and non-surgical healing have been enjoying a tremendous growth.

One reason, of course, is that they work. Not all healing produces miracle cures, and in some cases patients will have relapses or even die. But in all cases where healing can be called successful, there is some dramatic change of attitude on the part of the patient. A successfully 'healed' patient may still die, but he or she will die in a better, more positive frame of mind.

To the complete materialist – one who believes that there is nothing after death and that human beings are just a complex arrangement of chemical molecules and genetic inheritances – healing which results in death will of course have no purpose. Given the prevailing ethics of our present society, it can be difficult to realize that there is a difference between dying happily and dying full of anger and resentment. If there is nothing beyond death, then it hardly seems to matter whether we die in a positive frame of mind or in a state of rage. But for the growing number of people who believe that our method of dying will, in some sense, determine the nature of our next birth, then of course there is no comparison, and that is why so many people seek the solace of spiritual healing.

LAYING ON OF HANDS

This is the simplest and oldest type of healing. In a sense, it is practised by everybody. If a friend or relative is upset, we often put a hand on their shoulder in comfort. This act in itself may have some 'healing' power, even though the person laying on the hands may not regard themselves as a healer. Often, when we go to see people who are gravely ill in hospital, we will hold or touch their hands. This will not in most cases reverse their illness, but it will make them feel better for a time. It is a sign that the visitor cares, is sympathetic. All sympathetic and comforting human contact is, in a way, a laying on of hands.

Mothers apply this type of healing to small children. If a child comes in with a cut or grazed knee, the simplest healing treatment is to 'kiss it better'. The point about 'kissing it better' is that there is some transfer of energy which actually does make the child feel better.

But the laying on of hands by a professional healer goes far deeper than just enabling somebody to feel better. The transfer of energy can actually set in motion the healing process, and bring about dramatic changes. Most spiritual healers will use their hands, although they do not always lay them directly on the patient. Bruce McManaway often just passed his hands over a patient's wounds, and this was sometimes enough. People would often say they sensed a feeling of heat when McManaway's hands passed over the troubled spot. For McManaway, his hands also acted as diagnostic agents, sensing where the trouble was and sending out energy and love to that area. In his book *Healing – the Energy That Can Restore Health*, McManaway says that the concept of laying on of hands does not fit very comfortably into our present Western ideas of healing, as nobody knows exactly what is happening. He says that the 'placebo effect' must play a part, but that it should not be discounted as being any less effective than taking drugs or undergoing surgery. So long as the healing works, he asks, does it really matter *how* it happens?

Very many healers use their hands to sense where the problems are, and although the National Federation of Spiritual Healers does not allow actual diagnosis, sensitive hands will enable the healer to tell where there is disharmony, where the energy field is out of true. The basic objective of laying on of hands is not just to administer comfort and reassurance, but actually to counteract irregularities and restore balance and harmony in the body and mind.

Although hand-healers work on the body, and most do not ask questions about a patient's mental state, all believe that they are basically working on the level of the mind. With their hands, they are somehow reaching to the patient's consciousness and helping it to be healed.

Hand-healers may put their hands on the patient's shoulders or head, or move their hands down the spine – very many spiritual healers believe in the importance of the spine. As the healer touches various parts of the body, or passes his or her hands near the source of the problem, the patient will very often experience a sensation of heat. The healer's hands themselves may feel hot. If the healer is competent, the sensation of heat, which may be noticed when the healer's hands are near the trouble spot, will be accompanied by a definite feeling of relaxation and lessening of tension. It has now been proved by biofeedback techniques that all ill people have increased tension, so one of the first things a healer must do is to help the patient to lessen this; only when tension and anxiety have been released from the system can healing have a chance.

When healers use their hands, what exactly are they doing? At the very simplest level, they are employing the 'bedside manner' – showing the patient that they are one human taking an interest in a fellow human being. At another level, according to Bruce McManaway, some kind of beneficial energy is being made available, through the channel of the healer's hands, for the patient's benefit. Although the energy is transferred from the healer to the patient, this does not mean that the healer's own energy is depleted. Patients should be very wary of any 'healer' who seems tired and drained after healing sessions.

Although hand-healing works mainly on the mind – some healers say they are tapping into the aura which surrounds all humans, or the etheric body (there are various names for this non-material aspect, which, it must be said, has not yet been shown on machines to exist) – there is no doubt that physical improvement, often on a dramatic scale, can be effective. The late Harry Edwards, for instance, who was primarily a hand-healer, restored very many seriously ill people to abundant health simply by laying on his hands.

Chapter 2 talked about how the brainwaves of healer and patient must synchronize in order for healing to take place. Hand-healers are able to induce an altered state of consciousness and relaxation in their patients, using their hands as instruments. But laying on of hands is ultimately self-healing, as the healer can do no more than to try and enable the patient's own natural healing powers to be set in motion.

Healers usually start by placing their hands near the patient's head. No pressure should be exerted. Healers who are members of the National Federation of Spiritual Healers are advised to ask mentally for permission from the patient's higher self to begin the session. When permission has been granted, the patient becomes relaxed and receptive.

The healer should then scan the patient's seven major energy centres to see if they need balancing. These energy centres, or chakras, to use the Sanskrit term, are located near the brow, the throat, the heart, the solar plexus, the abdomen and the base of the spine. Those who have 'healing hands' should be able to pick up energy flows from these centres, and sense whether any are out of balance. All the time, healers should be asking themselves whether a paticular centre is losing energy, or being overactive. Energies come down through the top of the head and circulate through the chakra system. An experienced healer will be able to sense these and open them up, so that cosmic energy can flow through.

FAITH HEALING

This kind of healing is often confused with spiritual healing, and the terms are frequently used interchangeably. But in fact there is little similarity between the two. Spiritual healing works, or doesn't work, independently of whether the patient has faith in the healer.

In a more specific sense, the term 'faith healing' is used when talking about the kind of healing performed in the Bible, and is a belief that faith in Jesus Christ can bring about healing. If you put your faith in the Lord, so the belief goes, then He will heal.

Christian Science took this idea a stage further, and held that if you believed strongly enough in your own powers of recovery, then you could be healed. It is for this reason that Christian Scientists do not willingly use orthodox doctors, nurses, drugs, hospitals or surgical procedures – they believe in the power of faith, and the power of the individual to recover by means of faith.

Mark Twain cynically defined faith as 'believing what you know ain't true.' If you don't really believe in faith healing, then of course you won't be healed, but you do not have to have faith in God to believe that healing without medical intervention is possible.

Most spiritual healers maintain that it is not necessary for patients to have 'faith'. The healers themselves must have faith, of course – not necessarily faith in God, but faith that they can help the patient, that they can harness healing energy and help the healing process to be set in motion. In other words spiritual healers must have faith, or at least a firm belief, in themselves – otherwise they could not carry on healing.

In more modern parlance, faith healing is known as the placebo effect; and in modern medicine, the placebo effect is very necessary.

Although laboratory drugs are pharmacologically active and have definite therapeutic effects, whether we believe in them or not, our belief in them is what to a large extent affects their ability to work. If we go to the doctor, are given a drug and told that this will clear up the trouble, as often as not it does. If we go to the doctor saying we can't sleep and are given pills which, we are assured, will 'knock us out', then we will probably get a good night's sleep.

As patients we also invest a lot of faith in orthodox doctors. In our society we put medical students through a rigorous seven-year training, and it is a measure of our belief in them that, once they have qualified, that we pay them well and reward them with high social standing. In fact, the high standing of doctors is out of all proportion to their curative or healing abilities. But we reward them well because we have faith in them.

We also have a naïve faith that 'science' will be able to heal us. The magic words for any new product or drug are that it has been 'scientifically tested.' Many doctors, sceptical of the powers of natural medicines to heal, ask: where are the double-blind clinical trials? We have double-blind faith that any chemical or compound of chemicals which has been through this magic process of a large-scale clinical trial will have the power to heal.

When tested, very many 'natural' medicines on sale are found to be basically inert substances – but even so, people who have taken them for certain conditions often swear by them. Tranquillizers lose their power on our bodies after about two weeks, but they still produce a definite effect in people who take them. We all know that if you think something will do you good, then it often will.

It is also possible, to some extent, to think oneself into either health or illness. Many 'gentle' cancer treatments nowadays concentrate on visualization, which means seeing your body as healthy and tumour-free, or, alternatively, envisaging healthy cells fighting and overcoming the diseased ones. Clearly, you have to have faith in visualization in order for it to work. But you do not have to have faith in a spiritual healer for this type of healing to work. As most effective healers say: 'I've got enough faith for both of us'.

American magician James Randi has been looking into the claims of faith – as opposed to spiritual – healers, for forty years, and says that everywhere he goes he sees people being robbed of money, health and emotional stability. In his book *The Faith Healers* he writes that every disease has a natural variability, and that most patients seek unorthodox treatment when ordinary doctors have not been able to help them. He has come to the conclusion that faith healing is a method of 'useless treatment without harmful effects'. It will often appear to be effective as it makes the patient feel better, but usually has no effect whatever on the progress of the disease.

Randi says that, in investigating modern faith healing, he came across every method of technical, psychological and physical chicanery that could be imagined. He reserves his greatest condemnation for faith healers who make huge sums of money from plying their trade; in America, money made from healing is banked tax-free. Randi came across many examples of faked miracles, but no genuine cases of complete healing. He comes to the conclusion that the American public are being duped on a huge scale, and says he did not come across one 'healer' who could provide him with impartial evidence of successful healings.

Why, asks Randi, do so many Americans turn to faith healers when it is only so much 'high-powered quackery'? He maintains that faith healers are afraid of any rational scientific evaluation of their claims, and that they succeed in convincing patients that they are pawns in some cosmic game that the patients cannot understand. Randi is of the opinion that miracles are not being achieved, and that faith healers have no real powers.

He says there are two basic classifications of illnesses brought to both faith healers and orthodox doctors: imaginary ones and real ones. Some illnesses are completely psychosomatic, he says, and will appear to respond to faith healers. The 'real' illnesses are mainly the chronic ones – migraine, arthritis, allergies, multiple sclerosis, ME, asthma, eczema – all of which often go into remission, so the success of any 'healing' is hard to prove one way or the other.

Randi allows that what is called the 'endorphin effect', whereby a positive attitude sets the body's own healing and painkilling powers into action, does provide a better environment for healing. But basically he does not believe that faith healers achieve any lasting or discernible good at all.

Of course, it must be remembered that Randi set out with the intention of exposing the faith healers, and so it was on the cards that he would find what he was looking for. The question we have to ask ourselves is: are all doctors, nurses and alternative practitioners to some extent 'faith healers'? For, although the subjects of James Randi's investigations – who included such famous American names as Oral Roberts, Peter Popoff, A.A. Allen, Leroy Jenkins and a host of lesser luminaries – did not seem to produce satisfactory healings, it has to be remembered that very few orthodox doctors produce complete cures, either. But if doctors or medical science cannot cure a disease, it is labelled 'incurable'. The concept of faith healing is clearly very complex, and cannot be dismissed by investigations into a few Americans who practise dubious business methods.

SPIRITUALIST HEALING

This form of spiritual healing involves the help of discarnate entities. When spiritualism began in its present form in 1848, following some allegedly paranormal events which happened round the American Fox sisters, it was concerned mainly with contacting discarnate beings.

Over the century and a half that modern spiritualism has been in existence, very many famous and powerful mediums have come forward. They include Eileen Garrett, Leonora Piper and also Harry Edwards, who believed he was healing with the aid of spirit guides. Present-day spiritualism concentrates more on healing than anything else, and the majority of church services include a healing session; most of the work of spiritualists at the British headquarters in Belgrave Square now concentrates on healing.

Spiritualist healers believe that, when they heal, they are contacting long- or recently-dead real people who have now departed into the spirit world, and have thus acquired more wisdom and refinement than they possessed on earth. Sometimes these guides were American Indians in a previous incarnation, such as White Eagle and Silver Birch, and sometimes they were famous doctors or physicians.

Spiritualist healers believe that they act as a channel for the healing energy provided by their spirit guides. Usually, though not always, it seems as though the spirits choose a particular medium and work only through him or her. Usually spiritualist healers have no knowledge of medicine or diagnosis, but heal purely through the input of their spirit guides.

Spiritual healers will go into a trance, and it is only when they are in this state that healing can take place. Once in a trance, they are taken over by their 'controls'. Over the years, a great deal of investigation has been carried out on spiritualists, and their claims have been minutely researched, mainly by members of the Society for Psychical Research. In many cases, instances of chicanery and fraud have been discovered, and these have invested spiritualism with a kind of wicked glamour and a feeling that, although some mediums may be genuine, the movement as a whole is not to be trusted. But anybody currently seeking membership of the Spiritualist Association of

Great Britain has to provide evidence that they really are in touch with spirits. The SAGB is very concerned that its members should, like Caesar's wife, be above suspicion.

Spiritualist healing is currently very popular, and psychologists have often investigated mediums claiming contact with spirits, to see whether they are actually round the bend. Some psychologists have maintained that those who are able to go into a trance are probably suffering from schizophrenia, delusion or the complicated problem known as multiple personality. A Dr William Brown hypothesized that the two 'controls' who spoke through medium Eileen Garrett were actually aspects of her own personality. Accordingly, he subjected her to hypnosis and psychoanalysis in an attempt to contact these guides. He failed to contact either Abdul Latif or Uvani, Eileen's main controls, and in the end had to ask her to go into trance. Then, and only then, were the guides contacted.

Spiritualist mediums maintain that when in trance they are taken out of their bodies, which are made available for the personality of the spirit guide. It seems that normal consciousness is blanked out, and many mediums have no idea at all of what is being said during the trance state. When the medium comes out of trance, he or she rarely has any recollection of the event, which seems to be similar to deep hypnosis.

The renowned American healer Edgar Cayce was able to go into a trance, and it was during these altered states of consciousness that he could diagnose and prescribe for his many patients. When not in trance Cayce knew nothing of medicine and could not even begin to diagnose; but during a trance he possessed an enormous and accurate medical vocabulary, words which he had never even heard of consciously. The treatments Cayce prescribed were often highly unorthodox for the time, and he died of therapist's burn-out in 1945. Now, reading through the vast amount of literature he left, doctors say he was decades ahead of his time – some of the cures he prescribed are only now being discovered and used. Cayce explained his amazing powers by saying that in trance his conscious mind was able to contact his unconscious, and this was aware of the patient's condition. Edgar Cayce's gifts and powers have still not been satisfactorily explained, but there was no question of fakery.

Trance states are different from the condition known as multiple personality, as the controls or guides do not intrude into the medium's everyday life. The trances are deliberate, and happen at set times. With multiple personality, the 'other' intrusions are uncontrolled and involuntary. When a medium is taken over temporarily by a guide, there is only a wish to help and heal, never to perform demonic acts, as sometimes happens to those suffering from multiple personality.

The question remains for sceptics: do mediums really contact spirits from the 'other side'? There have been many theories, but as yet nobody really knows the answer, mainly because it is not usually possible for anybody else to contact the same guide. Spirit guides have a habit of choosing one person only, and when that person dies the spirit guide usually fades away as well. It could be that mediums really are contacting long-dead spirit guides. After all, nobody has yet disproved it conclusively.

Alternatively, spiritualist healers may be in touch with the energy that all spiritual healers can access, and they are giving this 'an earthly [or unearthly] habitation and a name', as Shakespeare says in A Midsummer Night's Dream. It could be that the 'spirits' supposedly contacted are simply manifestations of the higher energy which seems to be necessary for non-medical healing to take place. But then, some questions become difficult to answer. If spiritualist healers are not really contacting genuine entities, how does somebody like George Chapman's 'Dr Lang' fit in?

When he was first contacted by Dr Lang, when working as a fireman, Chapman carefully checked out all the information and found that there was such a person who corresponded exactly to all the data given him by the supposed spirit. Chapman himself has had no medical training, and yet is able to perform remarkable healing acts when in trance and taken over by Dr Lang. To date, there has been no satisfactory explanation of George Chapman's abilities other than that he really is in touch with Dr Lang.

Those who accept reincarnation have two answers as to what might be happening when mediums appear to contact those who have passed over. One is that the spirit is recently dead, and has not yet reincarnated. But that would not explain the phenomenon of Dr Lang, who died in 1937, after George Chapman was born. Perhaps he is still between incarnations.

Another explanation given by reincarnationists is that when mediums appear to be contacting long-dead spirit guides, such as American Indians who lived thousands of years ago, they are actually in touch with one of their own previous, more elevated lives.

Spiritualist healers say that when they are at work there is cooperation between the incarnate and discarnate bodies, and that is why healing can take place. Many of them work by using laying on of hands for the transfer of healing energy.

SPIRIT HEALING AND PSYCHIC SURGERY

As all terms for this kind of healing are rather similar, it becomes difficult to separate the various methods employed by healers to effect their work. As we have seen, spiritual*ist* healers call on their spirit guides in the other world to help them heal patients on the earthly plane. Spiritual healers call on divine energy to aid them with the work of healing, and are aware of a spiritual dimension to pain and suffering. Most spiritual healers do not use spirit guides, although some do.

But spirit healing, whereby a healer actually performs operations under the supposed guidance of a long-dead doctor, is slightly different again. Here, as we have seen in the case of George Chapman and Leah Doctors, the healer goes into trance, and the essence of the doctor in the spirit world somehow enters the consciousness of the healer, and performs 'spirit' operations.

The Rev. Dudley Blades, author of *Spiritual Healing: the Power of the Gentle Touch*, believes that our 'spirit friends' play a part in all healing. This, he says, has nothing to do with 'spiritualism', as healing always comprises teamwork involving both incarnate and discarnate entities. We all have spirit helpers, whether or not we realize it, he says, and when we invoke spirits we are tapping into the power supply of angels and archangels.

The so-called psychic surgeons in the Philippines have been subjected to considerable research and scientific investigation.

Alfred Stelter, a German chemistry lecturer who later specialized in parapsychology and paraphysics, spent nearly a year studying these paranormal healers. He witnessed the paranormal pulling of teeth and decided that when it worked it was a true paranormal action, in that no physical effort was needed to extract the tooth, and there was no pain felt by the patient; but equally he found that many attempts by healers to pull teeth just didn't work. Dr Stelter also witnessed the paranormal removal of an eyeball without any instruments being used.

Some paranormal healers perform 'spiritual injections', where the healer reaches in the air for a hypodermic needle and then 'charges' it by placing it on the Bible. The needle, of course, is imaginary and does not exist. Dr Stelter himself received a 'paranormal' injection on one occasion, and reported that blood came out from where the imaginary needle had entered.

Other healers in the Philippines can, apparently, produce cuts on the skin of patients by jerking their fingers about an inch above the skin. A razor-type cut appears and often quite a lot of blood. Sceptics have said that the cut is actually made by a knife or razor when the patient is not looking, but Stelter was certain that, on some occasions at least, the cuts were genuinely paranormal. His investigations also led him to believe that Filipino healers can paranormally open the body. They can, Dr Stelter maintained, dematerialize flesh so as to expose the bone, and then materialize it again. He says he saw Tony Agpaoa do this.

One of the problems with Filipino healers is that they often seem to lose their powers when confronted with Western scientists or Western laboratory conditions. Researchers have observed that, in order for paranormal surgery to take place, the healers have to be extremely strong mediums, and they must have a very deep religious belief and an undeveloped, uneducated intellect.

Dr Sigrun Seutemann, who is both a medical doctor and a psychic, has also observed paranormal healings. She took blood and tissue specimens produced through paranormal means by Tony Agpaoa and sent them to a laboratory. In some cases, the lab confirmed that these were indeed specimens of human blood and tissue, but in other instances was unable to offer such confirmation.

She also investigated the effectiveness of such 'healings' on 1200 patients who had come from the West for treatment by Filipino healers. Her conclusions were that 2 per cent of patients were healed instantly (about the same success rate as at Lourdes); 10 per cent had improved at the end of a two-week stay in the Philippines; 30 per cent experienced partial success; 30 per cent felt better after three months, and partial improvement was confirmed by medical tests; 18 per cent could not be followed up; and 10 per cent experienced no improvement at all.

Dr Seutemann says that she never witnessed the 'miracle' of a paralysed patient being able to get up and walk and dispense with their wheelchair. Most MS patients showed only a small amount of improvement, although a few, she says, showed considerable improvement. However, she does not state whether this was temporary or permanent. Terminal cancer carried on unabated. Kidney stones were sometimes removed by paranormal surgery, and the healing process was accomplished far more quickly than with orthodox surgery.

She says, though, that the state of mind of the patient who travels to the Philippines in the hope of a paranormal cure is quite different from that of the patient who is admitted to hospital. The travellers are expecting something extraordinary, and it is clear that the power of suggestion, faith, placebo, whatever, plays a very strong part. Dr Seutemann's conclusions are that paranormal healing can sometimes work, but in order for it to be properly understood people must realize that human beings are composed of mind and spirit, as well as body.

The conclusions that the many researchers have come to is that nowadays, whatever may have happened in the past, Filipino healers do not normally open up the body. The red liquid and tissue produced by 'operations' may sometimes be genuine, or it may be produced by sleight-of-hand and be animal, rather than human blood and tissue. It seems as if the powers of Filipino healers to perform spirit operations and extract body matter are declining as these people are being investigated. In any case, it appears from the research undertaken so far that, when successful healing takes place, it is more likely to happen in much the same way as spiritual healing – that is, by an exchange of energies, rather than by wondrous abilities to dematerialize flesh.

For further details of psychic surgery see Chapter 2.

SCIENCE OF MIND HEALING

Science of Mind, recognized as a religion in the USA, was founded in the 1930s by Dr Ernest Holmes as a way of bringing science and religion together. It seemed in those days that science and religion were at opposite ends of the scale – one was rational, objective, provable, whereas the other was nebulous, resting on blind faith, subjective. Dr Holmes' brainchild is not affiliated to any particular religion, but teaches that everything in the universe is basically spiritual. If we want to be healed, and to stay well, we have to accept this as a fact. We also have to accept that all illnesses are caused by negative states of mind.

Louise L. Hay, an American practitioner of Science of Mind, has written a booklet explaining the mental causes of illness. Her own realization of the power of this form of healing came when she was diagnosed as having cancer of the vagina. She says that, since she was raped and abused as a child, it was hardly surprising that cancer manifested itself in this area. She worked with a healer to clear up old patterns of resentment, as she terms it, having been given three months by her doctor to use an unorthodox method; he had recommended radical surgery as the only way of saving her life. At the same time she went to a nutritionist and learned how to detoxify her body through the right diet. Within six months, the cancer had gone. Louise says:

> *When a client comes to me, no matter how dire their predicament seems to be, I know if they are willing to do the mental work of releasing and forgiving, almost anything can be healed. The word 'incurable', which is so frightening to so many people, really only means that the particular condition cannot be cured by 'outer' methods, and that we must go within to effect the healing. The condition came from nothing, and will go back to nothing.*

It does not matter, she says, how long we have held negative patterns or a particular illness – we can begin to make a change today. If we sincerely want to be well, we must work to eliminate the mental cause of our illness or disease. If we are suffering pain and disease, she points out, at some level we must have a need for it. Science of Mind healers concentrate on helping their patients to release the need for the illness, for cigarettes, for alcohol, or whatever. 'When the need is gone,' writes Louise Hay, 'the outer effect must die. No plant can live if the root is cut away.'

The mental thoughts which create most disease in the body, according to Louise, are criticism, anger, resentment and guilt: feelings of low self-esteem, held long enough, will result in arthritis; anger turns into conditions which burn and infect the body; resentment becomes cancer – the body eating away at itself; guilt also leads to pain.

In her booklet she compiles a long list of ailments which she says have specific mental causes. Abscesses, for instance, are caused by fermenting thoughts over hurts, slights and revenge. Acne breaks out when we dislike ourselves, AIDS when we suffer sexual guilt and feel we are not good enough. Anorexia is extreme self-hatred and fear. Arthritis comes about when we feel unloved. Asthma is unresolved guilt. Back problems mean a feeling of lack of support in life. Bad breath means anger and thoughts of revenge. Baldness is caused by fear and tension and trying to control everything. Birth defects are karmic – you chose to come that way. Blackheads appear when we feel dirty and unloved. Bladder problems are caused by anxiety.

High blood pressure results from unresolved emotional problems, and BO from not liking ourselves and having a fear of others. Car sickness comes about from a feeling of bondage, of being trapped. Chronic disease is the sign of a refusal to change, and excess cholesterol from a fear of accepting joy and clogging up the channels of joy. Diabetics have a longing for what might have been, and a great need to control. They have no sweetness left. Earache means you don't want to hear. Epilepsy is caused by a sense of persecution and rejection of life. Fatigue results from boredom with what one is doing. Gynaecological problems represent a denial of the female self. Fevers represent anger burning up. Grey hair comes from stress, growths from nursing old hurts rather than letting them go. Headaches are a sign of a self-critical attitude. Heartburn comes from fear. Herpes is a sign of belief in sexual guilt and the need for punishment. Flu comes from a response to mass negativity and a belief in statistics. Kidney problems are a sign of criticism and disappointment. And so the list goes on.

Of course, such 'causes' for illnesses can only be asserted, never proved. But we do know that there are still very many illnesses for which nobody knows the cause. ME is one: although doctors and scientists have tried to find a virus, they have not succeeded, and at the time of writing the cause of this illness remains unknown to medical science.

Louise Hay states that children and animals often become ill because they are extremely sensitive to vibrations and atmospheres around them. Science of Mind healers concentrate on helping people to go beyond the physical to the metaphysical, and see themselves as loving, positive, perfect, suffused with love and energy. Then, according to practitioners of this twentieth-century religion, they can be well again.

HEALING SHRINES

The best-known healing shrine is Lourdes, where St Bernadette reputedly saw a vision of the Virgin Mary. There are many others, all related to visions of the Virgin experienced by children and young girls. La Sallette in France is just one of over seventy supposedly miraculous healing springs. Other well-known healing shrines are at Fatima in Portugal, Knock in Ireland and Medjugore in Yugoslavia. Although thousands of sick people annually make a pilgrimage to Lourdes, very few are ever healed. For many years now, a medical bureau at Lourdes has checked out all the claims for miracle cures and subjected them to exhaustive investigation: the findings are that there were only eleven attested cures between 1941 and 1956. The Catholic Church tells people not to expect a healing miracle from a visit to Lourdes, but the fact is that most people who go (who are usually, although not always, Catholics themselves) make the pilgrimage in the hope of a cure. Numerous researchers have observed that, although people do get out of their wheelchairs, throw away their crutches, their glasses or whatever, the effect is usually only temporary.

The Rev. Dr Leslie Wetherhead, a famous Methodist minister, investigated the Lourdes phenomenon and came to the conclusion that, as a healing shrine, its success rate was negligible. Only 2 per cent at most of its visitors experienced any effective or long-term healing, and even in those cases it would be difficult to say categorically that the cure was due to a visit to Lourdes.

The story started in 1858 when Bernadette Soubirous, aged fourteen and living in very poor circumstances with her family, was sent to a godmother in the country for her asthma. One day on a hillside Bernadette saw a vision of the Virgin, and it changed her whole life. She decided to become a nun, but she never really recovered from her asthma and died at the age of thirty. The importance of the vision, according to Catholics, was that it was a manifestation of the reality of spirituality.

Recently British pain therapist Ursula Fleming decided to investigate Lourdes properly, and to see whether there was any long-term healing possible from a visit there. In the autumn of 1989 she took nine patients, all suffering from a variety of serious and chronic complaints, for a three-week stay. With her were many helpers and two Catholic priests. She said:

As a long-time Roman Catholic, I've never come across anything at Lourdes which could be termed therapeutic. Most people go for pilgrimages and expect a miracle, but they never have therapy. The people I took all had very serious problems. One had a brain tumour, another very serious multiple sclerosis, one was nearly blind, one was arthritic, one had severe post-operative pain.

The idea was that these patients would go to Lourdes not expecting a miracle, but to see whether daily therapy, in the setting of Lourdes, could do anything to alleviate their problem. They had to accept the intervention of the spiritual, but back this up with modern therapy. While at Lourdes, they all had psysiotherapy, relaxation classes and pain therapy.

One of the first things that became apparent was that all the sick people were full of anger and resentment. So we were all working on helping them to bring about a change of attitude for the better. These patients had to learn emotional pain control, and to understand that negative emotions create tension and this in turn brings about illness.

At Lourdes, we were able to put people in a situation where they could realize that, by relaxing, their pain would be released, and that pain always gets worse if there is tension. It is true that illness is the result of disharmony, but that disharmony can have many causes.

The normal reaction of people to pain is to fight it. At the bottom of our fear of illness and our reaction to pain is a fear of death. I felt that Lourdes was in itself a very spiritual place, and that it might provide the best environment for these people to improve. But of course the real test of any healing is not whether people have become better in the protected situation, but whether they can carry this into their normal everyday lives.

Usually, people spend a week at Lourdes and come back absolutely shattered. They go hoping for a miracle but rarely do any work on themselves. To me, spiritual healing is perfectly possible and there can be some miraculous element, but I'm concerned to try and make it more efficacious and positive for more people. Fear of illness always comes back to fear of death, and it is only when this can be dispelled that healing can take place.

Fleming, who runs a private pain control clinic in London, is somewhat contemptuous of people who call themselves spiritual healers.

To me, it is disgustingly egotistical to call yourself a healer, as people always heal themselves given half a chance. The main danger for spiritual healers – and I'm not denying that many do have extraordinary powers – is that personal ego will come in. If as a spiritual healer you get a kick out of what you ar doing, it can become dangerous.

It is for this reason that I am concerned to put healing into a long-established tradition, such as Catholicism. Tibetan healing works in the same way. Nobody who was a real Catholic or a real Tibetan Buddhist would call themselves a healer. Healers are using psychic energy which anybody can learn to do, and which can be used for good or ill. I'm sure Rasputin could heal people if he wanted to, but he also performed a lot of evil as well.

When the people I took to Lourdes realized that their anger had a lot to do with their continuing illness, they understood why they were not well. During the three weeks they were there, they had learned a method of coping with their own pain, both physical and mental, and were able to start healing themselves.

ABSENT HEALING

Most spiritual healers, and spiritualist ones come to that, work not only by contact, or in the presence of the patient, but also with absent healing. Absent healing means that a healing message can be sent over many miles, and it will be picked up by the recipient in much the same way as television or radio can be picked up from long distances. It is possible for a healer in Britain to send out absent healing to somebody in Australia, and the energy will be picked up.

The National Federation of Spiritual Healers offers some information on absent healing in one of its leaflets:

Absent healing is done by spiritual healers, either individually or in a group, who attune with the Divine source to beam healing energies to the patient. This treatment is at a level beyond the physical and evidence shows that it can be very effective, particularly in the treatment of young children in cases of mental illness and in drug and alcohol addiction.

Most healers believe that absent healing is quite different from either faith healing or prayer, although undoubtedly prayer can be a form of absent healing. Ivan Cooke, founder in 1936 of the White Eagle Lodge, (dedicated to promoting understanding of spiritual healing, meditation and yoga, and named after the supposed spirit guide who inspired his teachings) believes that effective absent healing is the ability of a person or group of people to become attuned to the power of 'healing angels' which can be directed to those in need. It is not a question of blind faith, he says, but an exact science which can genuinely work.

Kenneth Cook, a chiropodist from Bridlington, North Yorkshire, was rushed into hospital in agony in February 1990. The doctors diagnosed a kidney stone, and said that he would have to stay in hospital for an operation to remove it. They took X-rays, on which the stone – about the size of a one pence piece – was clearly visible. Kenneth says:

I have been interested in spiritual healing for the past seven years, and do some chiropody work at a healing sanctuary. Kath Huddleston, who runs the clinic, and her team of healers promised they would send out absent healing to me while I was in hospital.

Soon after I was admitted the doctors and nurses started getting very worried, because my temperature had gone up from 37 to 39 degrees and they assumed I was developing some kind of infection. But I had already felt tingling in my fingers, and am certain the raised temperature was the healing coming through, as I had no infection of any kind.

I was taken into hospital on the Friday, and on Monday they got me ready for surgery. Before I went under with the anaesthetic I had the sensation that Children of Light were spraying me with silver light. The operation was scheduled for 10.30, and at 12.30 I woke up and started pulling myself together.

The doctor came to see me and said he couldn't understand it at all, as when they started looking for the stone it simply wasn't there. Yet it had quite clearly shown up on the X-ray. Kidney stones do sometimes dissolve in the urine, and the hospital staff watch your urine very carefully. But mine hadn't come out that way – it had simply disappeared and was, apparently, nowhere.

The upshot of it was that, instead of staying in hospital to recover, I was out on Tuesday afternoon, completely better and back at work by Thursday. The doctors did not believe in spiritual healing, but could not understand what had happened.

Very often animals, too, have been cured with absent healing. Animal healer Sylvia Crystal Broadwood gets requests from all over the world to send out healing to sick animals, and has had many letters from vets saying that the animal has miraculously improved. Mrs Broadwood feels that animals can often respond to absent healing even more than people.

The NFSH again has specific guidelines for effective absent healing. First of all, the healer must be in the right state of mind, and prepare the 'healing channel' – that is, open himself or herself up to the healing energies of the non-physical world. The healer must then visualize the body getting rid of all negativity and being peaceful and still. The next step is to visualize light streaming down and suffusing the body, and being absorbed into the body. The healer is then ready to give out absent healing.

This is done by speaking the patient's name aloud and releasing it into the atmosphere. The nature of the illness should not be mentioned – it is not important. Once the name is released a telepathic link is formed, according to the NFSH, and thoughts can then travel at the speed of light. When healing energies have been sent out, the session is brought to a close by the healer or healers drawing energy down into the feet. The healers should then rub their hands and knees and have a good stretch.

The main effort made in absent healing is to visualize the patient being in perfect health and strength and bathed in beautiful light. The healer must never concentrate on the illness, or give it any space in the mind, as this will make the illness stronger. You just don't think about it. In fact, the purpose of all spiritual healing is to visualize the patient in pristine health.

Although many of us feel that absent healing is strange, we are all familiar – from horror stories and films – of people visualizing evil on others. Black magic, voodoo and certain kinds of witchcraft concentrate on sending out evil thoughts to somebody to whom harm is wished. Very often, an effigy or doll is created and pins are stuck into it. Absent healing is the 'good' side of this ability. If we believe that black magic can work, we must also believe that absent healing has a chance of working.

In Chapter 3, reference was made to the 'absent healing' of plants. Although very few laboratory-controlled experiments have been conducted on absent healing, it seems from this one small experiment that there is at least something in it.

There is no need to be an accredited healer to be able to send out 'healing vibrations'. The late Ena Twigg, one of the most famous mediums of her day, recommended people at her many public lectures to send out loving thoughts whenever they passed a hospital or prison, or any other place which houses the distressed, the sad or the sick.

What if the patient does not pick up the vibrations you are so kindly sending out? After all, spiritual healers commonly say that patients can only be healed if they want to be – if they themselves become attuned to healing vibrations. The answer to this seems to be that patients will respond, even if they are not aware that healing is being sent out to them. The strength of the response does depend to some extent on the willingness of the recipient, but it will work unless the patient is consciously sending out anti-messages – which is unlikely to be the case, spiritual healers maintain.

Absent healing can be applied to many healing techniques – see, for instance, Radionics below.

RADIONICS

This is a form of diagnosis based on 'energies' supposedly emanating from the sick person. Although radionics has been in existence for over fifty years it has still not gained complete respectability, possibly because orthodox scientists cannot see how it can possibly work.

It all started in America when a Dr Albert Abrams, a neurologist from San Francisco, discovered that tapping on a patient's body produced a specific dull sound when the patient was suffering from certain conditions, and also facing west. Dr Abrams wondered whether this dull sound might be caused by some kind of electromagnetic radiation emanating from the patient.

He also discovered that this same sound could be reproduced when volunteers held flasks of diseased tissue. The next step was to attempt diagnosis by connecting patients to diseased tissue samples by means of a variable electrical resistor. Through these tests, Dr Abrams came to feel that certain diseases could produce particular electromagnetic radiations which could be picked up through modern machinery. He then hypothesized that, if the disease could be picked up on a particular vibration, it could be cured by another vibration.

Dr Abrams developed what has come to be known as the 'black box', which allows practitioners to tune into the patient's condition and then project a 'biocurrent' to cure the condition. The patient does not need to be present for the diagnosis to take place: a sample of hair, or nail clippings placed on the black box, would give an accurate enough reading of the condition.

The idea of radionics caught on quickly in America, and later practitioners invented special boxes which could diagnose illness by translating disease wavelengths into electrical ohms. As time went on more complicated machinery was invented, including cameras which could, it was alleged, take photographs of human organs at long distances. In Britain, the idea was taken up by George de la Warr, a civil engineer who had been asked to make some 'black boxes' for people interested in radionics – they had been unable to purchase the machines from America because of the difficulties occasioned by the Second World War.

The boxes consisted principally of a set of dials, and their development became de la Warr's life work. His later machines used what came to be known as a 'stick pad'. A thin sheet of rubber was stretched over a metal plate under which was an oblong cavity. The radionics practitioner would stroke the rubber lightly with his fingers while setting the dials to different diseases and conditions. When the resistance matched the radiation emitted by the disease condition, the rubber stuck to the fingers and the diagnosis was confirmed. Before long, it was realized that patients could be treated by this 'stick pad' from great distances: the rubber pad could work just as well when the practitioner concentrated his or her mind on the illness. When concentration coincided with the correct diagnosis, the rubber responded. At least, that was the theory.

Radionics has had a rather rough ride. In 1960, George de la Warr was charged with fraud by a Miss Phillips, who claimed that she had been reduced to a nervous wreck by trying to operate one of the instruments. The judge, Mr Justice Davies, dismissed allegations of fraud, but could not see how the long-distance camera she was using could possibly be a diagnostic tool. De la Warr eventually won the case, but could not pay the costs. Another charge was brought against an American practitioner, Dr Ruth Drown, who had invented some of these long-range cameras. In America the verdict went against Dr Drown, on the grounds that her instruments were not scientifically valid. She was sent to prison and died the following year, 1965, aged seventy-two with her life in ruins.

Radionics operates on the belief that all illnesses are caused by imbalances in the etheric body or aura that supposedly surrounds us all. All spiritual healers work on the etheric body, and completely accept the existence of this invisible casing round the physical body. The theory of radionics is that energy patterns of various kinds are emitted in all forms of matter and that these patterns become distorted whenever there is negative emotion, physical illness, stress or tension. Of course radionics practitioners, in common with other spiritual healers, accept that all physical illness has a mental and emotional component as well, and that diseases of all kinds cause stress, tension and anxiety. They also accept that most illness is caused by negative emotion of some kind.

Unlike other spiritual healers, who work with their hands or intuition, radionics practitioners supposedly pick up negative vibrations with complete accuracy on their black boxes. Health, they say, is maintained when energy is flowing freely round the body. All negativity distorts the energy pattern and affects the vibrations.

Practitioners do not consider radionics a form of faith healing, or accept that any success they have is due to the placebo effect. The success of the treatment does not depend on whether the patient believes in the method. The only requirement, as with other forms of spiritual healing, is that the patient should genuinely wish to get well.

Many radionics practitioners use hair analysis. The patient sends a sample of hair, and this will be enough for a skilled operator to perform accurate diagnosis. When radionics first hit the headlines in the 1950s journalists decided they would have a bit of fun with it: they sent in samples of cats' hair and birds' blood, along with a list of phoney symptoms, to see what the black box would come up with. Many practitioners fell directly into the trap, diagnosing arthritis, heart disease, diabetes and other complaints from the samples of animal tissue.

Some doctors have researched radionics rather more seriously, and several have come to the conclusion that, in spite of the instruments, the wavelengths and so on, this method of diagnosis does not stand up to strict scientific investigation. It seems that, in order to work properly, the box has to be operated by somebody who is sensitive and intuitive – somebody with spiritual healing powers, maybe. George de la Warr's wife, Marjorie, had this gift, and was able to diagnose with uncanny accuracy most of the problems that were presented to her. But others had no success at all. De la Warr himself said that those who were materialistic in outlook would not get good results from the box. Many people can get no sense at all from the stick pad.

Radionics seems to work best for those illnesses which have a definite psychosomatic basis, such as ulcers, dermatitis, high blood pressure, cancer, arthritis, asthma and eczema.

The black box has not been accepted into orthodox medical circles as a diagnostic tool, and many people remain highly sceptical about radionics. Most scientists can find no rational or logical reason why it might work, as it seems to contradict all known scientific laws. This, radionics practitioners believe, is because the method works on the etheric, rather than the physical body.

KIRLIAN PHOTOGRAPHY

Like radionics, Kirlian photography has its adherents, but has never become quite respectable or accepted by the establishment. Invented by a Russian husband and wife team, Semyon and Valentina Kirlian, in the 1930s, it is a form of high-voltage photography which apparently can show up the aura around all living things – plants, animals and people. A high-voltage charge is passed across photosensitive paper, and the object placed on the paper shows up an area of light surrounding the object.

Kirlian photography has been used mainly for diagnostic purposes in humans: an 'ill' aura is supposed to be very different in form from a 'healthy' aura. Certain healers have been quite enthusiastic about Kirlian photography, and have used it to see whether their own auras could be shown photographically, and whether these would differ from other people's auras. Kirlian enthusiasts have maintained that bright auras mean health, and dull ones disease. Some healers have maintained that the aura seen on Kirlian photography is ample evidence of the existence of subtle, vital energies – the etheric body.

But scientific research into Kirlian photography has proved rather disappointing, and it has not proved to be the diagnostic tool that was originally hoped. Professor Arthur Ellison, Emeritus Professor of Electrical Engineering at the City University, London, has closely studied Kirlian photography and has come to the conclusion there is no real mystery about it. In his book *The Reality of the Paranormal* Professor Ellison says that, to somebody who knows nothing about electrical engineering, electrical discharge is as mysterious as the etheric body. He believes that no conclusions about the existence of the etheric body, or about the health or otherwise of the patient, can be drawn from Kirlian-type photography.

One researcher, L.W. Konickiewicz, believes that Kirlian photography can accurately be used for medical diagnosis. Under laboratory conditions he was able to show that Kirlian photography could show up cystic fibrosis. He obtained a high degree of accuracy in his experiments, but these have not been repeated, and certainly Kirlian photography is not used for standard diagnosis.

Many spiritual healers get on to difficult ground when they try to use high-tech methods to 'prove' there is such a thing as a human aura, or an etheric body. A few years ago, some Australian researchers tried to establish whether the human aura could be detected. The three researchers, from the Department of Electrical Engineering at the University of Adelaide, used a photomultiplier tube and found that certain parts of the human body emitted light radiation. The intensity of this radiation was variable, and changed with different people. The researchers were able to establish that emitted radiation was an attribute of all living things, and that dead matter of comparable temperature and size does not emit similar radiation.

Many people, the researchers said, claim to be able to see a person's aura, a kind of light 10 – 20 centimetres from the skin's surface. Some investigators have also said that there is a bioplasma surrounding living objects. The researchers postulated that, if an aura or bioplasma exists, then it should be possible to show it with suitable instruments.

Although low-level light radiation was emitted from living matter, the researchers were quite unable to detect any aura of the kind often allegedly seen by healers and psychics. It is questionable, they said, whether this light radiation is the same thing as an aura, and concluded that, if an aura does exist, it is not obeying known scientific laws.

The human aura is, of course, often represented as a halo around holy people. But this may well not be a scientific fact. Or it may be that instruments have not yet been developed which can conclusively show such an aura. After all, if a hundred years ago people were told that they would be able to see in their living rooms moving pictures of wars, earthquakes and other disasters halfway across the world as they were actually happening, they would not have believed it.

The comparative failure of cameras and other high-tech equipment to show us the human aura does not mean that it does not exist. On the other hand, talk of the 'etheric' or 'spirit' bodies may be all rubbish. At the moment, given our incomplete knowledge, we have to reserve judgement.

AURA HEALING

This is a well-established method of healing which purports to 'cleanse' the aura around people, and so help it to be balanced and harmonized in order to restore health. Of course, in order to perform aura healing one has to believe that such a thing exists.

Practitioners of aura healing believe that all living creatures are surrounded by a radiance which we can all begin to see with a little practice. Auras, say such healers, vary in density and structure and contain a number of colours which indicate the health or otherwise of the individual. Betty Wood, author of *The Healing Power of Colour*, says that our eyes frequently play tricks on us, and it is possible to imagine we see an aura when in fact we don't. The best way of sensing auric colours, she says, is to tune into your subject and try to get on to the same wavelength. It is essential to remain in a relaxed state – many people start to see auras when they become practised at meditation. Soon, she says, you will be able to sense the auras, even if you don't actually see them – it's a bit like sensing the atmosphere or 'vibes' around particular people.

The aura, says Betty Wood, is there to protect us from negative energies, disease organisms, thoughtforms and spiritual knocks and bruises. According to auric healers, all mind-altering and medical drugs will damage the aura and leave the physical body unprotected, a prey to evil influences. Auric healers can, they claim, diagnose illness purely from sensing the aura.

Red in the Aura means there is a lot of vitality and sexual energy, and that the person is an extrovert, outgoing and generous. Muddy or dark red colours indicate some kind of negativity such as hate or malice. If there is black in the aura, this denotes great unpleasantness. Red plus black means evil, hatred and cruelty.

A clear, bright orange in the aura denotes ambition and a down-to-earth person. Apricot indicates a kindly, well-balanced type of person and is a sign of energy. A lot of orange means an ambitious, worldly sort of person, healthy and outgoing.

Yellow can be seen in people's aura when they are concentrating, reading or writing. Yellow tends to come and go, and is a good colour to have in the aura as it denotes mental ability. If there is gold in the aura, this indicates spirituality in the thinking. Dingy, muddy yellows are not good colours to have in the aura as they indicate suspicion, jealousy and clouded thinking.

Green is also an energy colour, but can mean that energy is being drained. Certain clairyovants believe that a lot of green in the aura means a person has healing ability. But too much green can mean detachment and lack of interest in others.

Blue is a positive colour, and indicates integrity, sensitivity and a religious sense. The deeper the blue, the more spiritual the person. Again, a muddy blue indicates negativity of some kind.

Violet is not noticed in everybody's aura, as it is very much the colour associated with spirituality. Grey in the aura means either that the person is depressed or ill, or is just not very interesting or exciting. Silver is associated with lively people who may not be very reliable; it is considered an indication of mercurial qualities. Pink is a very positive colour to have in the aura as it indicates affection, kindness and gentleness. Brown is the colour of a closed mind, of a conventional person, and is not a good colour to have in the aura. White means that the person is most probably a healer, or at least clairvoyant and telepathic.

Colour and aura healing go together, and have been employed since ancient times. Many modern healers work with colour rays, which are in fact the colours of the rainbow. What happens here is that the healer visualizes all the positive colours of a particular ray and brings that visualization to bear on the condition of the patient. Sometimes crystals of various colours will be used to enhance the power of this type of healing. What colour healers are actually doing is working with the various principles of certain colours to bring about effective healing.

For example, red is regarded as the ray of will and power, vitality and energy. Some healers regard red as an effective healing agent in disease where the blood is affected — such as in circulatory diseases, anaemia and depression. The orange ray denotes energy and is a more practical version of the wild, energetic red. It is considered helpful for chest conditions and digestive ailments. The yellow ray is associated with intellectual abilities and creativity, and can be visualized to help people who are having trouble with their nerves or suffering from skin diseases. The green ray denotes balance, harmony and sympathy. As it is considered a soothing colour, it can help headaches and emotional disorders. Blue can be used to soothe and calm the mind, and is sometimes used by healers for cleansing and treating fevers and nervous complaints. The indigo and violet rays can be used for treating epilepsy, rheumatism and nervous complaints. These rays indicate calmness and spirituality.

Recently colours and moods have been closely investigated, and it is known that there can be a close correlation between certain colours and states of mind. Some colours induce a restful, calm state of mind whereas others can produce agitation, fear and unease. A bright yellow room, for example, can make people feel schizophrenic, whereas blue and green have been found to improve the atmosphere of tense board meetings. Restaurant chains have known for a long time that oranges and reds encourage people to eat up quickly and get out, whereas cool, pastel shades encourage diners to linger over their meal.

Colour healers tend to work on the chakras, the places in the body where etheric energy of various kinds is situated. Colours are used to balance the various chakras and bring them into harmony, in the belief that illness results when the chakras are unbalanced.

Colour and aura healing are very closely combined, as the purpose of most colour healing is to improve the aura, and help the patient to change it from a muddy, grey-brown colour (a potent sign of serious illness) to a healthy, clear colour emanating positivity. There have been very few studies of a scientific nature delving into colour healing, and at the moment it is not really possible to say for certain what power it may have.

REBIRTHING

Rebirthing is not exactly spiritual healing, in that it does not depend on an exchange of energies from healer to patient. But it is part of the same movement which says that if we want to be healthy in body and mind, we have to eliminate long-held negativities.

The idea behind rebirthing is that very many traumas and problems and chronic illnesses can be related back to a difficult or painful birth experience. Reliving one's birth, according to the theory, helps individuals to face these fears and to let them go. As rebirthing can in itself be an extremely traumatic experience, it has to be carried out with a properly trained therapist. Usually, the birth experience itself can be relived in one session, although several will often be needed in order to change chronic negative patterns of behaviour associated with a painful or difficult delivery.

The concept of rebirthing originated with Leonard Orr, an American psychologist who encouraged patients to hyperventilate to gain an altered state of consciousness. In this state the patients were asked questions which took them further and further back through their childhood. Some rebirthers ask patients to adopt a curled-up foetal position as gentle pressure is applied to the head and feet.

Rebirthing is sometimes known as primal therapy, a method of releasing long-held fears and traumas which was developed by psychiatrist Arthur Janov, author of *The Primal Scream*. Janov used rebirthing to treat certain neurotic states, in the belief that some people never really recover from not having their initial needs met by their parents or other carers. Janov encouraged patients to relive birth scenes until the trauma had been successfully released. Then, only the 'real self' is left.

The notion that certain birth experiences, such as Caesarean section, premature and forceps births, can lead to behavioural problems in later life has encouraged doctors and antenatal teachers to place a new importance on the life in the womb, and on the state of the mother and father before and after conception. Judith Collignon is a British rebirther who believes there is a direct correlation between the birth experience and personality in later life. She came upon this link by accident when she was working in America with delinquent children and went to see the parents of a child who was having severe behavioural problems at school.

During therapy the boy progressed to a certain extent, but Judith felt that something was being held back. Eventually, the mother told her that she had had a nervous breakdown during pregnancy because her husband had left her for another woman. She had seriously considered an abortion. Although she had not carried this through, she had spent the rest of her pregnancy wishing the child would die. When she learned this, Judith Collignon felt that the child realized at some level that he had not been wanted. When the child was told, he said that he had always known that somebody wanted him dead. But after the story had come out into the open the boy's behaviour began to change for the better and his school work showed a marked improvement.

Judith Collignon says:

I started looking into more cases, and the more I looked, the more apparent it became that the things that were creating the difficulty were often not early childhood, as was once thought, but the actual birth experience. I now believe that the least interference and intervention there is at birth, and the more natural the whole process, the more likely the person is to grow up well-adjusted, healthy and non-neurotic.

Research has now shown that where there is no foetal distress, where the mother is conscious and not asleep, and can be with the baby, the children have better personalities, become more confident people, and feel loved and wanted. If the transition between being in the womb and coming out of it was safe and painless, then there will be better motor coordination, the child will walk and talk more quickly, and also be stronger physically. If a baby has a good start in life, there is always an inner feeling of confidence.

When there is a Caesarean birth, however, often the all-important bonding does not take place and that first link is missing. I have noticed that often women who have had Caesarean births themselves have a yawning need for affection which never seems to be met. This can be manifested in promiscuous behaviour. Such people are always trying to get love, and sex can become the most intimate form of bonding they know. Also, men who have come into the world by Caesarean births can find it difficult to establish a good relationship.

Touch is very important. Many of my patients have been premature babies who were put into intensive care units and never touched or held properly. We are now realizing that even very premature babies thrive on touch. Traumatic birth experiences are very common, and one reason why so many people have personality problems. But with successful rebirthing, these can be solved.

With rebirthing, we try to put people back in touch with their very first experiences, so that they can come to terms with them as adults. Then you can transcend the problems and let them go.

HYPNOSIS

Now becoming very respectable, hypnosis is widely used to treat addictions such as smoking, nervous complaints and conditions such as irritable bowel syndrome. In some cases, it is now available in Britain under the NHS.

The development of hypnotism in some ways parallels that of spiritual healing. There is some evidence that the ancient shamans and priest-healers used a form of hypnotism to effect healing, and that hypnosis was also used in the healing temples of ancient Greece.

But modern hypnotism owes its origins to Franz Mesmer, inventor of the term 'animal magnetism' (and from whose name the term 'mesmerize' is derived), who used a form of laying on of hands to bring about an altered state of consciousness in his patients. Mesmer believed that 'animal magnetism', or as we would term it, healing energy, could pass from him to his patients with dramatic effect. Simply by gestures Mesmer used it to induce convulsions and catatonic states in his patients.

By the 1820s it was being demonstrated that patients could be put into a trance, in which state they would feel no pain and could be operated on. This was, of course, before the days of anaesthetics, and the 'magnetized' patients, who would normally be screaming in agony, would lie quietly and apparently painlessly while the operation was being performed.

Since this seemed to contradict known scientific laws, as spiritual healing does today, the medical profession would not believe that the patients genuinely did not feel pain. The doctors were convinced that they were specially trained by the magnetizers to pretend to feel no pain. There was no way, they argued, that 'animal magnetism' could be transferred from the therapist to the patient – indeed, there was no such thing as 'animal magnetism'. So how could there be such a thing as hypnosis?

James Baird, a Scottish physician of the time, decided to investigate mesmerism with a view to exposing it once and for all. But he discovered to his surprise that animal magnetism was a reality, and that it actually was possible to hypnotize people and put them in a trance. It was Baird who first used the term 'hypnosis', which soon came to replace the word 'mesmerism'.

In previous investigations of mesmerism, doctors had been convinced that, if an altered state was achieved, it had something to do with occult practices and was therefore evil – something aligned to witchcraft. Baird tried to put the whole business on a scientific footing, saying that the altered state of consciousness induced by hypnotists was simply something which could happen to everybody's nervous system. There was nothing occult or shamanistic about it.

Once effective forms of anaesthetic, such as ether and chloroform, had been discovered, enabling surgeons to perform operations painlessly, the original role of hypnotism was no longer relevant. But hypnotism did not die out. During the later half of the nineteenth century, a number of doctors in France used the technique to suggest to their patients that their condition was now better. They had such success that eventually hypnotism was used to treat hysterical and nervous conditions.

Sigmund Freud worked a lot with hypnosis, following his visits to the French hospitals where hypnotism was a standard form of treatment. Later, though, Freud came to feel that hypnosis could not be part of satisfactory psychoanalysis, as patients had to be conscious and have proper recall at all times. He discovered that hypnosis did not always help patients to uncover what they were repressing.

Gradually hypnosis died out as a therapeutic tool employed by doctors and psychiatrists and became part of stage shows and quackery. During the first half of the twentieth century all forms of hypnosis had a very bad reputation indeed, and at best were reduced to a form of entertainment, not to be taken seriously.

It was not until the 1960s, when all forms of alternative and complementary medicine began to be taken more seriously, that hypnosis and hypnotherapy were revived as healing tools. Even today many orthodox doctors frown on hypnotherapists, whom they castigate as unqualified quacks. But gradually doctors themselves are now learning to hypnotize, as it is increasingly being found that, for some diseases, hypnotherapy is the only treatment which works.

It has been said that not all people are susceptible to hypnosis – and that no hypnotist, however clever, can take over your mind and make you do things that go deeply against the grain. Hypnosis is basically a form of deep relaxation which induces the alpha state in the brain. As the Mind Mirror has shown, effective healing, of both mind and body, must take place at the alpha level. Hypnotherapists are people who have acquired or learned the ability to induce this alpha state into other people. But if you deeply resist going into this state, then there is little the hypnotist can do.

Sometimes patients will be put into a deep trance, in which they become completely unaware of what they are saying or doing. When such people are brought out of hypnosis, they remember nothing. While they are in a deep trance, their unconscious thoughts may rise to the surface. Hypnotism can be used either to access repressed states or to cure organic conditions, such as digestive problems and warts.

Hypnotherapists usually begin a session by taking a full medical history, and discovering whether the patient really wants to be cured of the condition. If not, then the hypnotist will be wasting his or her time. The whole point of modern hypnosis is not to make unacceptable suggestions to the patient, but to lessen fear, anxiety and tension so that the healing process can be set in motion. In this, hypnotherapists are not very different from spiritual healers – they are just using a slightly different means to effect a recovery. Most spiritual healers do not induce trance states into their patients.

Hypnosis works partly by the power of suggestion and partly by the induction of a relaxed state. But as with any other form of healing, unless patients are prepared to change the attitudes and lifestyle which brought about the illness in the first place, then the condition is likely to return. Very many people have found that the power of hypnotherapy to help them give up smoking, for instance, has only a temporary effect – because deep down they wanted to go on being smokers.

It seems that hypnotherapy is most successful in dealing with disorders which have an underlying emotional cause, such as stress-related problems, high blood pressure, asthma, migraine, insomnia and ulcers – in other words, conditions which cannot as yet be successfully treated by orthodox medicine. Hypnotherapy is becoming ever more popular as these conditions are on the increase. British GP Dr David Ryde has for many years successfully used hypnosis to treat stress-related conditions, and says that he has found hypnotherapy particularly effective in those cases where ordinary treatment simply doesn't work: blushing, bedwetting, phobias, relationship and work problems and nervous disorders of various kinds.

Hypnosis is now widely used both for dental treatment and childbirth, as it is being realized that anaesthetics bring with them their own problems. There are several stages of hypnosis, from simple relaxation to a really deep trance after which the patient does not remember anything. The deep form of hypnosis is used most often for deep-seated emotional problems. But it has to be remembered that, even when deeply hypnotized, the patient is not asleep and may regain ordinary consciousness at any time.

This is in fact a safeguard for the patient. It is virtually impossible for hypnotists to suggest to the hypnotized patient wicked things that the patient will then act on. Apart from the fact that just one such case coming to public attention would completely destroy the hypnotherapist's livelihood, there is always the possibility that the patients may slide back into consciousness. The trance state is not stable, and may be broken at any time.

Hypnosis, in common with other forms of non-drug healing, can help patients to have a more positive attitude towards themselves – it can be employed to impart confidence and self-esteem and to keep the body and mind healthy. Hypnosis cannot be used for learning foreign languages and acquiring other difficult knowledge easily and painlessly. Although successful hypnosis may help people to recall languages and information they once knew, they will only ever recall what they have already learnt consciously. Hypnosis cannot put things into the brain: it can only bring out what is already there, or help negative attitudes or addictions to disappear by positive suggestions.

Basically, hypnosis is a form of treatment whereby the conscious (beta) mind is suspended for a time and suggestions can go straight to the unconscious, which is more receptive to the power of positive suggestion. As Freud said, the unconscious cannot accept a negative. Hypnosis can enable people to bring to the surface traumatic or even pleasurable memories which may have been buried. Recalling these experiences can in itself be a healing process, and relieve the deep-seated emotional problem which has been causing ill health in the present.

PAST LIFE THERAPY

This is a form of treatment, allied to spiritual healing, through which patients troubled by phobias or problematic conditions are gently regressed into a previous life. In order for past-life therapy to work, there has to be a strong belief on the part of the therapist that there is such a thing as past lives. A few years ago most ordinary, medically trained psychiatrists would have laughed at the very idea that traumas adversely affecting the present could be related to something which happened in a previous incarnation. Now, although mainstream psychiatrists still believe the idea is nonsense, a number of avant-garde practitioners in Britain and America are using this method of healing with great success.

Past-life therapists believe that it is not always possible to trace a particular condition or disease back to something which happened in this life. There are very many mental and physical illnesses, they say, which defy all medical intervention and therapy. Phobias are a prime example. A phobia may be defined as an irrational fear of something which is not inherently or not invariably harmful, such as spiders, knives, snakes, flying in an aeroplane or being in a confined space. When treating phobias, ordinary therapists can very often find nothing at all in the present life which could have caused the fear. With fear of flying, for instance, a very common phobia, it is extremely unusual for the phobic to have had a bad experience or an accident when in an aircraft. In fact, most people who have an irrational fear of flying have never been inside an aeroplane at all.

Yet if such a person can be regressed back to a past life, then very often, according to past-life therapists, the cause of the problem will be found. Somebody who has a severe fear of flying in this life, for instance, may have been killed in an aeroplane during the First or Second World Wars. Somebody who has an irrational fear of injections may have been killed by injection in a previous life. Somebody who has an abnormal terror of fires may have been burned at the stake.

It is not necessary for the patient to believe in reincarnation to be successfully treated by past-life therapy. The treatment will work independently of belief. Some hypnotherapists specialize in regressing people through hypnosis to a past life. Joe Keeton, a well-known hypnotherapist from Liverpool, has had many successes in treating phobias and anxiety states through past-life regression.

Medically trained psychiatrists who use past-life therapy believe that their method of treatment goes back further than standard Freudian psychoanalysis. Whereas Freud believed that many behavioural and emotional problems in adult life could be traced back to repressed childhood experiences consciously forgotten, past-life therapists say that not all problems have come with this present life and some go much further back. Most of these psychiatrists use hypnosis to help people remember their past lives; it is not usual for these to be recalled except under hypnosis. And usually, once the hypnotic session has ended, there will be no memory of what has been said when in a trance state.

Past-life therapists are looking for clues to what caused the present problem. It is not always a matter of phobias, although these can seriously blight people's lives. Some people have extreme difficulty in forming relationships. Some have morbid dreads, or anxieties, which cannot be related back to any experience at all in this life. Some people are full of fear. Yet others are plagued by hate, resentment and jealousy, and blame their parents for not having brought them up in comfort, love and luxury. By delving into past lives, patients can be helped to see what has created negative or non-useful patterns of behaviour in this life, and to extricate it by means of understanding.

Sometimes, a greater understanding of past lives and of how bad or wrong patterns may have been created will help the patient to come to terms with present circumstances, and to have a more positive attitude.

Past-life therapy is growing in popularity all the time, as the idea of reincarnation takes hold once more in society. Most, if not all, spiritual healers believe in reincarnation, as they say there is nothing else which can explain the sheer diversity of humanity, and why there are so many ills and disease states which seem resistant to cure. Basic to past-life therapy is the idea of karma, which says that we ourselves have created the conditions we are born into. We should not blame our parents or society for giving us a rough deal; nor should we blame ourselves. It is our karma which has created the present conditions, although past karma does not have to affect the present adversely. By understanding their own karma, people can be helped towards a more positive future.

An objection which has often been raised in connection with past-life therapy is that it is difficult, if not impossible, to prove that the accumulation of past lives has caused the present problems. After all, with emotional problems which started in childhood it is usually possible to check whether rape or abuse, for instance, took place, or whether a parent walked out when the child was one or two years old. It is also very often possible to establish what kind of birth a patient had. But with past-life therapy it is more or less impossible to prove one way or the other that the present patient was once a Second World War pilot, burned at the stake as a witch, or fatally stabbed during a duel, for instance.

The only way that the success of past-life therapy can be assessed is whether it makes a dramatic difference to the person's life, and improves things out of all recognition. If severe phobias suddenly vanish, or negative states of mind are turned round to become positive attitudes, then in a sense it doesn't matter whether the past life actually happened or not. As detractors say, it is never possible to establish beyond all possible doubt whether the patient under hypnosis is recalling a genuine personal memory, or merely remembering a book or film which made an impact at the time. With past-life therapy, the proof of the pudding has to be in the eating.

Those opposed to hypnosis and past-life therapy often ask: if we really did have past lives, surely more of us would remember them? But most of us would have a job to recall what happened last week, let alone last century. Few of us can remember what we did when we were two years old, and certainly nobody can remember being born. But the fact is that we *were* all born, and we *were* all once two years old. So the absence of memory does not in itself rule out the reality of past lives.

SOUL-DIRECTED THERAPY

This is a specific form of spiritual healing developed by Dr Lisa Sand, a psychiatrist, and Inga Hooper, a psychic and a medium. They work mainly with patients who are schizophrenic or suicidal, who suffer from deep anxiety, stress and depression. Both Dr Sand and Mrs Hooper, who practise in Sutton, Surrey, believe that, in order to be well, the body, spirit and mind all have to be addressed.

Dr Sand is a Jungian psychiatrist who believes that most disorders, including physical ones, derive basically from a sickness and disharmony within the soul, the non-physical aspect of humans, and so she concentrates on this aspect rather than the body. She says that in most cases a single session is enough to restore health, and is as effective as several years of psychoanalysis.

The sessions start with Inga Hooper giving a clairvoyant reading and getting mental pictures of long-repressed childhood events. Both Dr Sand and Mrs Hooper believe in reincarnation, and Mrs Hooper very often gets intimations about patients' past lives and their influence on the present incarnation.

After the clairvoyant reading Dr Sand will discuss what has transpired with the patient, asking whether any of this is recognizable. Very often, she says, recognition happens at once and is followed by a strong reaction which can start the healing process in motion. Once long-held fears and anxieties are released, says Dr Sand, they can no longer contribute to disease in the body.

Sometimes, soul-directed therapy can be emotionally painful, as it asks patients to confront aspects of themselves and events which have long been buried or repressed. But while they continue to be repressed and unacknowledged they are causing harm, and mean that the patient is less than optimally healthy.

SOUL-DIRECTED ASTROLOGY

This is a form of spiritual healing practised by Mary Russell, a psychologist and daughter of two doctors, who works closely with Lisa Sand and Inga Hooper (see above). Mary Russell believes that a person's birth chart can give an accurate blueprint of all their tendencies and aspirations for this particular incarnation. Like Dr Sand and Mrs Hooper, she has come to believe in reincarnation.

Russell uses astrology because she knows, she says, that it works.

I believe that the movement of the planets in relation to each other and to the earth can map out the development of humanity. I was scientifically trained, and at first astrology seemed like complete nonsense. But now I believe that it has a scientific basis. In my work, the birth chart has been proved right so many times that it seems the most accurate tool that I can use.

It's basically a starting point and something to refer to when I am talking to the patient. It's my belief that all disease, mental, emotional and also physical, begins with some disharmony in the soul, and that unless you address this, you are never going to be properly healed.

I don't tend to see people with serious physical complaints so much as those who feel there is something badly wrong in their lives, that their lives lack direction or love or ambition, or that they can't seem to make anything work. I also see a lot of people suffering from stress-related and nervous complaints and depression. The point is that, unless the nervous complaints can be sorted out, serious physical disease will inevitably follow.

When potential patients get in touch with Mary, she asks them their date and time of birth so that she can draw up a chart. Then she asks them to come and see her.

The main trouble with most people who come to me is that they haven't been able to build up a sense of self. They don't know exactly who they are or what they want. Their birth chart can help me to see which directions they should be aiming at. I try to help them to see what feels right for them. I am not a guru and I don't give advice. I think that would be wrong.

Sometimes one session will be enough, but other patients will need two or three appointments before their lives can proceed in a more positive direction. 'I am trying to heal through astrology', Mary says.

I see my job as healing the split between the spirit and the personality. I believe that the soul is more than the subconscious. As I see it, we have all been through very many lives and have many aspects to the soul. Once the split has been healed, and the disharmony brought into balance, then the improvement is usually permanent, as people have a flash of recognition about themselves.

Mary Russell insists that not everybody is a suitable candidate for healing. 'Some people are harbouring very negative emotional material, and they can be absolutely blind to what is wrong with them.' Some people who believe in reincarnation are against the idea of healing, as they say it is interfering with people's karma. She answers this by saying:

When people come to me, it is their action and their choice. I always wait until somebody asks – otherwise it would be interference and unjustifiable. I would never say to anybody: let me help you. I would never canvass for patients, or suggest that somebody comes to see me. They have to want to change something in themselves, and also be ready for change.

But the changes themselves can be difficult and painful. Not everybody is willing to make them, and in those cases healing can only ever be temporary. Unless you are prepared to work hard to change your life, the same problems will inevitably come back to haunt you.

THERAPEUTIC TOUCH

This form of non-drug healing was developed mainly by Dr Dolores Kreiger, Professor of Nursing at New York University, who became interested in the possibilities after reading of Dr Bernard Grad's experiments with mice and healers. (see Chapter 3). After conducting her own mini-trial with Colonel Estebany, Dr Kreiger was convinced that there was 'something' in healing, and that healers genuinely could influence the constituents of blood.

Dr Kreiger terms therapeutic healing a marriage between an ancient technique and modern science. Her belief is that anybody can practise therapeutic touch, and that special psychic or healing powers are not needed. Basically, therapeutic touch is a way of inducing the relaxation response into people so that healing can take place. Dr Kreiger does not believe that therapeutic touch can replace medical science but feels that it should work in conjunction with it. Accordingly, the nurses she trains have all been taught this form of laying on of hands.

The 'touch' consists of feeling for the patient's energy field, and then 'unruffling' this by means of stroking. In order to transmit the healing energy the sender must be in a state of calmness and relaxation. Unless the sender is relaxed, there will be no transmission of healing energy.

In common with other healers, Dr Kreiger states that it is most important that the healer should be aware of his or her own motivation. Because there is necessarily a close link between healer and patient, damage can result unless the healer has good intentions. There should be love, and a genuine wish to help. Ego must not get in the way. Dr Kreiger insists that ultimately it is self-healing, and all that the therapeutic touch can do is to set this process in motion. Therapeutic touch has proved particularly beneficial for reducing pain and anxiety in childbirth.

MODERN CHRISTIAN HEALING

Although healing of course goes back much further than Christianity, most of us are more familiar with the healing miracles of Jesus Christ than those of any other healer. But for very many centuries Christian priests and ministers did not practise healing, believing that was something best left to doctors.

In recent years, however, there has been a major revival of the Christian healing ministry, and there are now several residential centres and day healing sanctuaries where people can go for Christian healing and laying on of hands. There is a very definite concern among a growing number of believers that Christianity is in grave danger of losing all its spirituality, and that churches are fading into cosy social clubs which have no real meaning or influence in the outside world.

Julian Drewett is secretary of the *Churches' Fellowship for Psychical and Spiritual Studies* and editor of its journal, *The Christian Parapsychologist*, which reminds Christians of the spiritual roots of their religion. He says:

> *There is no doubt that Christ's healing miracles actually happened, but there have been attempts in recent years, among Christians themselves as much as anybody else, to discredit and explain them in terms of known scientific laws. But we believe that there is a psychic dimension to life which must be addressed by Christians.*
>
> *As we see it, healing comes into this. Healing is definitely the act of transmitting something powerful from one person to another. The energy transmitted is neutral, and can be used for evil as well as good.*
>
> *We are in favour of healing in the name of Christ. In fact, Christ did encourage his disciples to go out and heal the sick, and this is what we should be doing as Christians. There is never any guarantee, of course, that people will always get better physically, but we should not be addressing only the physical side of humans.*
>
> *The fact that healing is now coming back into the Christian ministry is an encouraging sign that the spiritual tradition of Christianity is being newly recognized. You never get anywhere with a materialistic religion.*

The Old Rectory at Crowhurst in Sussex is a Christian residential home dedicated to Christian principles of healing, which basically comprise the laying on of hands. The former chaplain, the Rev. David Howell, explains specifically what Christians mean by 'laying on of hands.' The authority for this aspect of Christ's ministry, he says, is found in the Bible. The act of 'laying on of hands' is, according to him, the oldest sacramental action known to humans. The word 'sacrament' in this context denotes 'an outward, visible action which expresses an inner meaning'. So the act of laying on hands is the external expression of something that God is doing within us.

But healing, within the Christian tradition, is not the only means associated with hand gestures. A hand can be laid on somebody in the form of a blessing, or as a way of identifying with somebody. When a person is ill or troubled, we often put a comforting hand on their shoulder to show that we are in sympathy with them, that we have their welfare at heart. Very often, this act of touching somebody can be healing – especially if the person is extremely ill or has an infectious disease. Jesus, says David Howell, laid his hands on lepers – the outcasts of contemporary society, the people whom nobody would touch or go near for fear of being contaminated. Hands are also used in several Christian services, such as confirmation and ordination, when hands are laid on the candidates with an accompanying prayer.

'Although healing is not explicitly mentioned in blessing, identification or receiving of the Holy Spirit,' says David Howell, 'together they add up to healing in a very deep sense. To be assured of God's blessing, to know our Lord identifying with us through the hands of those who minister, to be filled afresh with the Holy Spirit – all this is healing indeed, and can be our realistic expectation when coming to a healing service.'

At the heart of all Christian healing, he says, is prayer; no real healing can be accomplished without it. Most Christian healing services are accompanied by a prayer which is said aloud. A typical one is this:

In the Name of the Father and of the Son and the Holy Spirit, we lay hands upon you that the blessing of God the Father might be upon you; the healing mercies of Jesus Christ the Son enter your spirit, soul and body; and the renewing power of the Holy Spirit be released within you at every level of your being. May the Lord take from you all that harms you, and fill you with his peace, joy and love; and may he restore you to useful service to the glory of Jesus Christ our Lord. Amen.

Those who lay on hands in the Christian context are not people who have proven gifts of healing, but are the ministers, vicars, rectors and bishops of the Christian Church. In a way, Christian laying on of hands is rather like the King's Touch: in past centuries the sick would queue up to be touched by the King in the hope that their diseases would go away. Some Christians, although not all, believe that those called to the Christian ministry have special powers and can therefore be effective when laying on their hands.

Healing can take place in a number of different ways. The commonest place to lay the hands is the head – the idea is that the healing energy and love of God will suffuse throughout the whole body. In certain instances, though, it may be more appropriate to touch the part of the body that is afflicted. Attendance at one healing service will not always be enough: sometimes sick people need several sessions before the healing process starts. David Howell says that in some cases Jesus had to lay on hands more than once for effective healing to take place.

Absent healing is also an aspect of the Christian healing ministry: ministers will pray for an ill person who cannot attend the service in person. David Howell says that there is no scriptural precedent for absent healing, but 'prayers of intercession' (for other people) are well known in Christianity. This has an echo, for instance, in the famous hymn *Eternal father strong to save*, which has as its chorus:

> Oh hear us when we cry to thee
> For those in peril on the sea.

'There is ample evidence,' says David Howell, 'that God honours this laying on of hands by proxy.'

'We cannot always know,' he adds, 'how the Lord will heal, but we are promised that in this ministry he will be at work. It is also important that we order our lives in a way pleasing to him, so that we co-operate with him in what he is doing.' Modern Christian healing is not so very different from any other form of spiritual healing, and is the Church's attempt to be useful in the modern world.

PART III

5 ✿ Self-healing

Ultimately, all healing must be regarded as self-healing. As Don Copland has said, all that even the best healers can do is to provide a kind of 'jump lead' which enables the self-healing process to be set in motion. Although spiritual healers may be able to transfer some initial healing energy, the rest must be up to the patient. And unless patients are willing to change their lifestyle for the better, then healing will be more or less a waste of time.

All healers say that people must sincerely want to get better, if their input is to make any difference. At first this may sound a strange thing to say, because surely everybody wants to be well? Surely nobody likes to suffer the pain and hopelessness of terminal cancer, the agony of chronic arthritis, the frustration of paralysis? Wouldn't we all prefer wonderful, abundant health and vitality?

In one sense, maybe, yes; but in another, deeper sense the answer may be no. If, as all spiritual healers maintain, disease and sickness come about through a deep disharmony within the soul, then getting well again will entail taking a long, hard look at oneself and making dramatic, far-reaching changes. This may involve some deeply painful introspection, and not everybody is willing to face this.

Learning to forgive
For instance, we now know that many physical illnesses can result from long-term emotional pain that has been suppressed.

Back pain, arthritis and cancer are examples of conditions that are very often caused by resentment, anger and hate being bottled up and never allowed an exit. This is not mumbo-jumbo but scientifically valid. Anybody who harbours negative emotions will inevitably start to suffer from stress. And stress, as has been shown, eventually means that physical organs will be affected. All doctors now accept this. But in order to release the resentment one has to forgive, forget and send out love to the one person or people who have caused the hatred.

This is not always easy to do. If, for instance, you have been sexually abused by your father, or were abandoned by your mother in early childhood, you are not likely to feel very loving to these adults who abused their position. So you go around with a burden of hate and anger. This burden, which causes chronic stress, may eventually manifest itself in some chronic physical problem such as migraine, a weakened immune system and susceptibility to infections, or skin complaints. If you were told by a spiritual healer that the only way of sending these complaints away was to forgive your father or your mother, and send out love to these suffering individuals, would you be willing to do it? Many people are not: they hang on to their hate, and do not see why they should forgive somebody who has caused them so much deep distress.

What we have to realize, say healers, is that we cause our own distress. Nobody causes it for us. Obviously as children we are utterly dependent on the adults around us, but when we are adult ourselves we can choose whether or not to be adversely affected by other people's negativity. As we cause our own mental distress, so we can, with help, un-cause it, and be healed.

Now of course 'healing' does not always mean that the body will become 100 per cent healthy. For example, somebody who has walked with hunched shoulders bearing a grudge all their life will probably never be completely straight – the bones will have grown in a deformed way. Sometimes the body is too eaten up with cancer by the time healing is sought for there to be a possibility of a complete recovery. The mind has to be healed first, and then the body will respond as best it can. But the body may have been subjected to years of drugs, chemotherapy, surgery, assaults of one sort or another, and be quite unable to return to a state of physical perfection. Sometimes the person will die – but that does not necessarily mean that the healing has been a failure. If a person dies peacefully and without pain then healing will have made a demonstrable difference.

Also, the lifestyle must support the healing. There is not a lot of point in seeking healing for lung cancer if you continue to smoke. Healing cannot over-ride the abuse to which some people subject their bodies. Smoking, drinking, taking mind-altering or illegal drugs and eating unhealthy food will all contribute to illness in the body. Those looking for healing have to realize that these are all ways in which deep self-hatred is being manifested.

The positive form of self-love

At one level, healing means loving oneself more. Once there is greater self-love, there will be greater respect for the body, and less of a wish to damage it by bad habits. If you love yourself, you want to treat yourself well.

Louise L. Hay, the Science of Mind practitioner who healed herself from terminal vaginal cancer, believes that self-love and self-esteem are essential for lasting health. In her booklet *Heal Your Body* she writes:

> *I love myself, therefore I take loving care of my body. I lovingly feed it nourishing foods and beverages. I lovingly groom and dress it, and my body lovingly responds to me with vibrant health and energy. I love myself, therefore I provide for myself a comfortable home, one that fills all my needs and is a pleasure to be in. I fill the rooms with the vibration of love so that all who enter, myself included, will feel this love and be nourished by it. I love myself, therefore I work at a job that I truly enjoy doing, one that uses my creative talents and abilities, working with and for people that I love and that love me, and earning a good income. I love myself, therefore I behave and think in a loving way to all people, for I know that which I give out returns to me multiplied. I only attract loving people into my world for they are a mirror of what I am. I love myself, therefore I forgive and totally release the past and all past experiences and I am free. I love myself, therefore I live totally in the now, experiencing each moment as good and knowing that my future is bright and joyous and secure, for I am a beloved child of the universe and the universe lovingly takes care of me now and for evermore.*

We cannot individually create a loving, peaceful universe, but we can learn to be loving and peaceful in ourselves. This idea is not, however, the same as being a doormat. Doormats are trodden on by others and get ill. Doormats are people for whom others have no respect. Doormats try to please other people: not themselves. That is why they become ill, as they find they can never please other people and that, instead of gratitude and love, they receive only insults and abuse. Illness usually comes about when people are confused and have no true sense of self – they do not know who they are, what they want, what they should be doing or how they should relate to other people. A truly peaceful and loving person is one who has great self-respect and self-esteem – an appropriate sense of self.

Most people only consider spiritual healing when they have something so badly wrong with them that it frightens them: they are going blind, they are worried about recovering from a major operation, they have had cancer diagnosed, they have a chronic and serious heart condition.

A need for sickness?
Spiritual healers believe that serious illness comes about when we have an important lesson to learn. If we can learn that lesson, we will become healed: if not, we will continue to get ill. It is noticeable, for instance, that people who seem to make a remarkable recovery from a serious illness very often go down with something just as severe not long afterwards. Many people who appear to have 'beaten' cancer find that a few years later the tumours start appearing again: this is because they have not become healed.

Very many people dislike hearing that their illness is 'psychological' and insist that it is purely physical. This attitude is very noticeable in the new (or newly recognized) illness of ME, or myalgic encephalomyelitis, where patients suffer extreme exhaustion for no apparent reason and wake up tired and drained even after fifteen hours' sleep at night. For many years most doctors dismissed this illness as being 'all in the mind', because they could not find anything wrong with sufferers. ME patients were often regarded as malingerers. Then, thanks to some ferocious campaigning on the part of sufferers, the disease came to be seen as genuine. Far from being malingerers, most sufferers from ME are high achievers, perfectionists, people who give a lot and who work hard in their professions. Recently doctors and researchers have started taking ME more seriously and began looking down their microscopes to find a virus which might be responsible. Now, ME patients are saying that their disease is caused by a virus and is purely physical, not psychosomatic; they are powerfully rejecting the label 'psychological' when applied to their condition.

Something similar has happened to sufferers from food intolerance. These people, who have a variety of extremely baffling complaints varying from chronic migraine to digestive and allergy problems, were also marked down as 'neurotic'. To describe these people's state doctors used the term TNS, or thick-note syndrome, meaning that their case histories were far more voluminous than those of other patients, but that whatever treatment was tried they never seemed to get any better. In recent years, we have learnt that bad diets of one sort or another can cause a multitude of 'psychological' disorders – hyperactivity in children, delinquency, severe mood swings, pre-menstrual tension, post-natal depression and even schizophrenia.

Susan Sontag, a ferocious opponent of the 'soul-is-sick' idea, says in her famous book *Illness as Metaphor* that illness is often seen as manifestations of neurotic states of mind until a cure is found. She cites tuberculosis as a prime example. In Victorian times, she says, TB sufferers were seen as having a whole host of personality disorders which made them prey to the disease. Then a cure came, and everybody just forgot about the 'TB personality'. The same, she predicts, will happen with cancer: when, eventually, a cure is found, the present ideas that cancer patients have a particular type of disordered personality will fade away and be forgotten. Sontag believes that we foist all kinds of complicated psychological conditions on to simple physical diseases, conditions which just disappear as soon as an effective cure is found. Making out that an illness has complicated psychological roots, she argues, simply gives it more importance and centrality than it deserves. Some doctors support these views.

So where does all this leave spiritual healing and self-healing? My belief is that there is truth in both approaches. It is true that we do tend to invest illness that we do not understand with psychological or non-organic origins. It is certainly also true that negative states of mind and apparent neuroses can be made better by altering the diet and giving appropriate supplements. It is the case that many ME patients are found to be harbouring a virus which has embedded itself deep in the system and cannot easily be extricated.

But, we have to ask: *why* is it that some people get ME when others don't, if the virus is lurking around all the time? *Why*, in a flu epidemic, do some people succumb and others not, when there is equal exposure to the germ? *Why* do some people get cancer and others not? *Why*, in Victorian days, did some people get TB while others, living in identical conditions and eating identical food, remained healthy?

For the answer to these questions, we have to look at our personal environment. Viruses and bacteria, like the poor, are always with us, but they will only flourish in fertile ground – where the defences are down, where the immune system is weak, where there is stress in a person's life. It is my belief that we attract viruses and infections to ourselves when, for some reason, we need to be ill. The reasons for this need are legion.

Some people may need to be ill because they want to escape responsibility for a bit, to put their feet up, to withdraw for a while from the fray. Others need to be ill because they feel guilty about what they have been doing. Yet others don't like themselves very much and don't feel they deserve to be well. Some people may want to punish themselves. Some may want to punish others. Certain people – mothers fall commonly into this category – want to be ill so that those dependent on them can realize just what is being done for them, and be grateful. There is a whole host of motives predisposing to illness, and all of us are prey to negative feelings at times, to crises of confidence, to feelings that we are not properly appreciated. It is whenever we allow negative feelings to take hold that we risk becoming ill.

We also have to take on board the fact that, although doctors and scientists do find effective cures and treatments for certain illnesses, we then just become ill with different diseases. TB has been more or less wiped out, it is true, but we've got food intolerance, candida, cervical cancer, breast cancer, hyperactivity in

children, PMT and many others in its place. The fact that cures
are always being developed does not mean that we are gradually
getting rid of illness and becoming healthier and healthier.

Some of us, of course, may be born with a 'strong constitu-
tion' and always be well, while others are sick and illness-prone
from tiny babies upwards. Spiritual healers believe that we
come into the world with a karmic burden from the past, and
that whenever bad handicap – or extreme privilege – manifests itself, that is the result of our past karma. Most modern
doctors and scientists scoff at this idea – but they have no other
way of explaining it except that there is a 'genetic' or hereditary
problem. But their explanation will not make the handicapped
or desperately ill person better, although spiritual healing
might, if it is possible to get through to the sufferer.

Self-help

Since, according to spiritual healers, we each come into the
world with our own unique karma, we will all succumb to different types of illness and have differing rates of recovery. But
we can always help ourselves if we want to. Not all of us will
have the power or strength to become spiritual healers of others,
but we can all become our own healers by employing some tried
and tested methods for non-drug, non-interventionist healing.

Effective methods of self-healing include: visualization,
meditation, learning to relax and positive thinking, all of which
have become very popular in recent years, and all of which
demand some effort from the patient. There's more to self-
healing than going to the doctor for a prescription and then
faithfully taking the pills. All spiritual healers maintain that in
the end effective healing is always self-healing, as it has to be the
person's own body and mind which bring about the healing
process. Other people never heal you.

VISUALIZATION

All that visualization really means is using the power of the
imagination to make yourself well. The term was first used by
the American radiologist Carl Simonton and his wife Stephanie

Matthews Simonton, who employed this method with terminal cancer patients. The idea became very popular in the early 1980s, and then faded somewhat, as it was found that terminal cancer patients very often didn't recover, even when they had made strenuous efforts to visualize their cancerous cells being invaded and killed by good, healthy cells. Visualization can never guarantee a return to perfect health, of course, but it remains a useful tool, not so much to reverse serious illness as to keep yourself well.

In Britain, two of the main exponents of visualization are Matthew Manning and Ursula Markham. Markham, who is basically a hypnotherapist rather than an actual spiritual healer, teaches visualization to the patients who come to her suffering from stress, migraine, back problems, addictions, nervous complaints of various kinds, and any disorder which can vaguely be labelled 'psychosomatic' or which the doctor can't seem to help.

In her book *The Elements of Visualization* she outlines what is meant by the idea. Visualization, she says, is not a substitute for medical care, but can work hand in hand with orthodox treatments to bring about a more effective and lasting cure. Unlike Christian Scientists she does not recommend self-diagnosis, or ignoring the medical profession and hospitals, or the use of visualization to cope with all pain. Very often pain is our signal that something is wrong, and to try to overcome it by 'positive thinking' may be the wrong approach.

Using visualization to remove pain is only sensible when you know exactly what is causing the pain, and you have sought all medical help possible. Pain therapist Ursula Fleming believes that usually we make pain worse by fear and by tension. Visualization can help long-held pain to disappear because it brings about the relaxation response and also enables us to use our imagination effectively.

Ursula Markham has three useful visualization tips for dealing with pain. First, imagine you are standing under a warm and gentle shower which, as it cascades around you, is taking away the pain. Another method that works for some people is to sit by the leg of a table or chair and, as you hold on to it, imagine that your pain is leaving you and transferring into the inaminate object instead. (This type of visualization is similar in some ways to Christ sending the psychiatric illnesses into the Gadarene swine.) Ursula Markham points out, though, that one of her patients could not bear to do this, as she hated the thought of her house being full of aching table and chair legs! A third method of visualization for dealing with pain is to sit in your most comfortable position and establish slow, regular breathing. Once this has become steady, imagine that with every inhalation clean, white air is going into your lungs. As you exhale, imagine that dark, painful air is being expelled. This visualization should continue until the air being exhaled is as clean and pure (in imagination) as the air coming in.

Although we can all practise visualization to keep ourselves healthy – we imagine ourselves being strong, well and resistant to infection, and reinforce this by saying; for example, 'I never catch colds' – for more serious illnesses, such as cancer, this method of treatment needs to be taught. It is one of the 'gentle' range of treatments used at the famous Bristol Cancer Help Centre, where patients are taught to see strong white blood cells attacking and overcoming the invading cancerous cells. In order to make the visualization strong enough to be effective, says Ursula Markham, cancer sufferers often need to imagine they have a battle raging inside them. Some patients imagine that knights on white chargers are coming along to defeat dangerous dragons. Others have visualized an army of cleaning ladies scouring away the stain inside their bodies. Yet others have visualized an internal vacuum cleaner sucking up all the bad cells.

Visualization has been endowed with a certain mystique because of its use in 'alternative' cancer treatments, but all it really means is the ability to see yourself as a well person rather than as an ill one. The act of visualizing yourself as healthy seems to reduce fear, as it means you are actually confronting your illness and facing it – coming to terms with it. It also means that you want to be well – if you don't, you will be unable to visualize effectively. Most of all, according to Ursula Markham, it allows patients to feel that they are taking part in their own recovery, and not being passive recipients of medical care. To be well, you have to take an active part in your own healing.

MEDITATION

At the beginning of the 1980s, heart specialist Dr Malcolm Carruthers coined the neat phrase 'meditation not medication' as the way forward in health treatments. Dr Carruthers, who had recently started practising a form of meditation known as Siddha Yoga, became convinced that meditation was the best way of solving health problems which had their origins in lifestyle rather than infections. At the time it sounded rather cranky, especially as this kind of meditation involved chanting, looking at pictures of half-naked Indian men and going into a kind of trance for an hour or so. But meditation has now proved itself an effective tool for dealing with many stress-related problems, mainly because it can bring about an altered state of consciousness, the 'relaxation response' which was so dramatically measured by Maxwell Cade on his biofeedback machines.

Meditation is, of course, a very ancient means by which humans have attempted to get closer to God. In modern terms it has been harnessed, like Western forms of yoga, as a healing tool which works whether you want to contact a god or not. Transcendental meditation, the method made famous by the Beatles' guru, the Maharishi Mahesh Yogi, has more or less dispensed with all the 'godly' aspects and focusses on learning meditation as a way of calming the self whenever stress threatens. Modern, Western meditation works on the belief that it is possible to calm yourself down with conscious effort, to alter brain rhythms and to stop the body from getting on 'red alert' when there is no need for this. Autogenic training is a form of meditation and relaxation specially developed for Westerners, and involves giving yourself instructions such as 'My left leg feels heavy and warm' to bring about this calm, relaxed state.

People often imagine that meditation is a form of daydreaming in which you go off into another world. In fact, both meditation and autogenic training, like visualization, require hard, conscious effort and have to be learnt. Some people meditate easily, while others find it extremely difficult and boring. Autogenic training has to be taught by an expert, after which it can be employed at any time when needed.

The point about learning to meditate is that all the body's arousal systems are calmed down so that the healing process can start to work. As we have seen, it is impossible to bring about self-healing while the body is in a state of turmoil and tension. Meditation, when performed properly, has the power to reduce the heart and respiratory rate, and to encourage brainwaves to go into the alpha or even the theta mode.

In order to bring about a meditative state, you must be in a silent, calm environment. Get into a comfortable sitting position. In the East, yogis meditate in the lotus position, but this is too difficult for most Westerners to achieve. If you are uncomfortable in your meditation position the relaxation response simply won't come about, and you will be fidgety and cross. Some meditation techniques use a mantra – a 'magic' word or phrase repeated over and over again. The reason for this is that repeating a mantra blocks out interferences from outside, stops unnecessary thoughts intruding and allows your imagination to get to work. Some people focus their eyes on a candle or other soothing object while they meditate – others prefer to meditate with their eyes closed.

Although meditation has become relatively mainstream over the past few years, there is still a great deal of resistance to it in orthodox medical circles, and also among patients, as it still retains an unfortunate link with seventies' drop-outs, drugs and a general lack of effectiveness. This is starting to vanish now, as businessmen and top executives are being taught meditation techniques to help them reduce stress and the build-up of tension in their lives. But the main problem with meditation, as with most self-help techniques, is that it is a skill which has to be learnt and then practised daily. At first it can seem very much like doing nothing – time-wasting, in fact.

Meditation, like relaxation and visualization, also involves facing up to one's illness, one's distress, one's life problems, and trying to tackle them at source. So many people prefer to ignore them, hoping that they will go away, or try to push them down into the deep recesses of the mind; but this only ensures that they will fester until they force themselves to your notice with an actual illness. It often takes a lot of courage to face up to one's own problems, and try to take responsibility for them. It can be much easier to go to the doctor for pills, which don't require a reappraisal of attitudes or beliefs. Cancer specialist Dr Alec Forbes, a co-founder of the Bristol Cancer Help Centre, used to say that, when he told patients that if they didn't alter their diet and habits they would be on pills for the rest of their lives, many would reply: 'Give me the pills, doctor.'

There is also antipathy to meditation because, to the casual eye, many practitioners seem to be rather fey, ill, distressed people anyway. And their consulting rooms often contain some huge kitsch illuminated picture of an Indian guru looking impossibly holy, which seems alien. But the reason for the pale and wan looks is that most people who practise meditation have to – they've been driven to it because of some great crisis in their lives, and have become ill and wan as a result. Detractors often muddle cause and effect. It's really only unfamiliarity which causes the problems – and the basic fear in people that they do not want to face up to the reality of themselves.

The average person will consider meditation only when there is a serious problem, when stress is threatening to destroy their health or livelihood, when there is severe pain or deep mental distress. As yet very few are using meditation to *prevent* ill-health, but it can actually be one of the most effective ways of setting the self-healing process in motion. It is one's own 'spiritual healing' kit which is always available.

RELAXATION

There's more to relaxation than flopping into a huge armchair with a glass of whisky by one's side and turning on the telly. Genuine relaxation is, ironically, hard work! It involves retraining the mind and the body in order to reduce stress and anxiety.

You can measure your state of relaxation if you have access to a biofeedback machine – but of course most people haven't. However, you can learn to relax without being wired up to machinery. Dr Chandra Patel, who has taught biofeedback and relaxation for many years, says that relaxation is rather like driving a car – simple when you know how to do it but even so a skill that has to be learnt. In order to learn to relax, she says, you must have motivation, understanding and commitment. You must genuinely want to know how to relax, and understand what you are trying to achieve – why you feel this need for relaxation.

Deep muscle relaxation is the best kind for bringing about the 'relaxation response' in the brain and for slowing brainwaves down to the healing level. For this you should have a quiet, warm, comfortable place where there is no TV on and the phone won't ring. Buy a relaxation cassette, and listen to the instructions several times before trying to follow them. (Some good cassettes are available from Ursula Fleming Tapes, see page 168.)

But there are also simple, everyday relaxation exercises you can practise to ensure that undue tension does not build up. For example, at red traffic lights release your grip on the steering wheel, take one deep breath and let your body relax. Do the one-breath relaxation whenever the phone rings – it will ensure that you will be calm and friendly when you pick up the phone. Whenever you are pressed for time, do this same deep breath. Dr Patel suggests making a list of ten situations that are likely to make you tense or upset, and then try to relax before they crop up. Practise doing this with minor tasks first, and then with more important situations.

Of course, the ability to relax does not mean that you will never become ill, but as healing can never happen unless there is relaxation and relief from stress, then it is a good idea to practise as much as you can. In any situation, the ability to be calm and relaxed will help to send away pain and fear.

Basically, self-healing entails a willingness to work on oneself, to replace all negative thoughts with positive ones, and not to dwell on hate, resentment, jealousy, possessiveness, greed and lust. The reason for this is that negative thoughts rebound on the thinker, not on the object of the hatred. All spiritual healers maintain that, before self-healing can be really effective, there must be a concept of the self as a basically spiritual being rather than primarily flesh and blood. There has to be a spirit of forgiveness to those we feel have wronged us in the past, other- wise we will carry a burden of resentment. There must never be any blame, attached either to oneself or to other people: mental self-flagellation migitates against successful self-healing.

We must also rid ourselves of any feelings that we are unworthy or useless. Women have to avoid being seen, and seeing themselves, as objects of men's desire – that too leads to illness as it focusses completely on the body. if a person sees you only as a body, they don't see the heart – and the only real communication between people is at the non-physical level. Buddhists say that the only real way to health and happiness is to eliminate desires from one's life – as soon as people are free from desires, according to this doctrine, they become mentally freed. If you believe you are a failure, then you cannot be healed. There have to be positive affirmations all the time. The main purpose of self-healing is to engender lasting emotional health, which will bring about good physical health as well.

Of course self-healing, or healing by a recognized healer, is not always an effective substitute for proper medical care. Some conditions do need drugs, surgery, hospital treatment and the expertise of specialists. But attitude makes all the difference to recovery rates, wound healing and the possibility of not going down with the same illness again. Sometimes people need the services of a spiritual healer in order to come to an understanding of what healing is all about.

But how do you find a good one? Are there lots of charlatans, quacks and get-rich-quick merchants in the growing business of healing, or are they mostly genuine people with definite powers and a strong wish to help others? This will be examined in Chapter 6.

6 ❦ Going to a Healer

If you are interested in consulting a spiritual healer, how can you choose the right one? How can you be certain that the healer you visit will be genuine, and will have definite healing powers?

Professional safeguards

A few years ago these questions might have been extremely difficult to answer, as anybody – in Britain at least – could set themselves up as a spiritual healer without having any powers or abilities at all. Now, with the establishment of the National Federation of Spiritual Healers, which currently has more than five thousand members, and also the Confederation of Healing Organizations, there are very many safeguards. Although it is still the case in Britain that anybody can set themselves up as a spiritual healer, those who are affiliated to the NFHS must abide by a definite code of practice and are pledged to work in close contact with doctors and other members of the medical profession. In addition, the Federation runs regular courses (as described in Chapter 1) where probationary healers can develop their gifts and learn the mechanics of present-day spiritual healing.

The National Federation of Spiritual Healers is not aligned to any particular religion and none of its members will try to convert you, or to dragoon you into accepting any doctrinaire set of beliefs. But the word '*spiritual*' does denote an important aspect of their work. All such healers believe that the fundamental causes of illness lie in disharmony and imbalance at the level of the soul, and that the healing energy they utilize comes from a divine source. Therefore there may be meditation, prayers, strange practices like 'centring' or a few moments' quiet contemplation before the session starts. Don't expect it to be exactly like going to the doctor.

What to look for in a healer

Some very successful – in the material sense – spiritual healers now have secretaries, receptionists and a whole host of personnel to attend to you. But if they have not, this does not necessarily mean that they are any less effective. Do, however, beware of practitioners who guarantee a cure or who ask for large sums of money in advance.

Spiritual healers do not advertise or tout for business: this is seen as very wrong, and completely contrary to the universal laws to which spiritual healers are supposed to be attuned.

A good spiritual healer will be extremely busy and may be booked up for several weeks ahead. Matthew Manning, for example, as mentioned earlier, has a nine-month waiting list; very popular healers such as George Chapman are also tremendously busy. But however busy the healers may be, they should never appear drained or tired. Healers can draw on a more or less limitless supply of divine, or cosmic, energy, and so they should not get tired. A good healer will know how to pace him or herself so that there is no undue draining, nor danger of therapist's burn-out. Healers have to make sure they look after themselves properly, so that they can be calm and peaceful for all their sessions. Beware of any healer who seems harassed or rushed: you are going, above all, to be bathed in an atmosphere of peace and stillness, not rush and stress. The atmosphere in a healing sanctuary should be the very opposite of that of a busy general hospital.

Spiritual healers should not attempt to diagnose complaints. They may ask you what is wrong with you, and take some kind of case history for their records, but they will not prescribe or seek to alter or supplant your medical treatment. Nowadays, spiritual healers are not particularly interested in what is wrong with you – that is not the point, as they are primarily seeking to help patients restore balance and harmony to their lives. To quote from an NFSH leaflet:

By laying on of hands, by attunement through meditation and prayer whether or not in the presence of the patient, a healer seeks to induce a beneficial effect upon a patient's life force at all levels of existence. Spiritual healing may be given for any illness, stress or injury as a therapy which has no side effects and is complementary to any other therapy. The medically diagnosed nature or severity of the illness is unimportant with regard to the outcome.

The right frame of mind

The most important aspect, as far as the patient is concerned, is that there should be a deeply felt need to be healed. Alternatively, in the case of absent healing, a request should have been made to the healer by a friend or relative. As a patient, you do not have to believe that spiritual healing will work, nor do you have to have faith in the healer. But you should not imagine, either, that the particular healer can perform miracles. Sometimes these do happen, but by their very nature they are rare. It is not fair to expect a spiritual healer to lay on hands for half an hour and miraculously cure you of all your ills. This may happen, but it is more than likely that it will not. Most healers say that they have around a 30 per cent success rate, as far as complete recovery is concerned.

But it will not help if you go in a sceptical frame of mind. It is important for all patients to have an open mind, otherwise there may be deep resistance to what the healer is trying to achieve and the session will be a complete waste of time for both healer and patient.

Your first session

When first going to a spiritual healer, you may be feeling strange, and as if you are doing something rather spooky. A good healer will be able to make the patient feel at ease, and normal. The healing room or sanctuary should send out a loving and warm atmosphere. Most spiritual healers will ask you to sit down and ensure that you are comfortable before healing begins. There may be soft music and candles, or there may be silence. But there should be an atmosphere of peace and calm in the healing room, which should not be used for any other purpose. The correct vibrations are an important part of the healing process. Patients who feel ill at ease or who are unable to establish any kind of rapport with the healer may not be able to gain benefit. At the very least, you should feel better just for being in the healer's presence. Sometimes, though, healers and patients may not hit it off – there is sometimes a clash of personalities, or of attitudes.

Edna Thorogood from Esher, in Surrey, was very conscious of the benign atmosphere when, at her wits' end, she decided to consult a healer. She had started to develop arthritis when she was fifty. Over the next five years her hands, ankles and feet swelled so badly that she became almost housebound. Her doctor could do nothing to cure her, and to alleviate the pain could only prescribe strong drugs, which Edna did not want. She said:

I was desperate. It had got so bad that my husband had to cut all my food up for me. I couldn't even turn a tap on. Then I saw an ad for a spiritual healing centre. I decided that I had nothing to lose, and went along to the centre, which is run by Jean Dreghorn.

When I rang to make an appointment, I said: 'My feet are a complete disaster. Every time I take a step it's like walking on broken glass.' She said they couldn't promise a cure, but that they would do their best.

As soon as I went inside the centre, I felt better. There was such a lovely peaceful atmosphere. The healer gently laid her hands on me, and instantly I felt a warm glow. In fact, it was more than a glow – it was an actual sensation of heat. From that first session the pain began to lessen, and after about two months it had gone altogether.

My doctor has followed my progress with interest, and is very open minded about spiritual healing.

Edna says she has experienced other benefits apart from regaining her mobility and the lack of physical pain.

I have a much more peaceful and harmonious feeling inside, and my general health has improved as well. When you have terrible arthritis, the pain actually drives you mad. There is no medical cure for the condition, and really, spiritual healing is the only thing that can help. I'd certainly recommend it to anybody – so long as you make sure you go to a reputable healer.

Most sessions last for half an hour, with an initial consultation lasting an hour or more. It is perfectly all right for you as the patient to ask the healer what training he or she has received, what qualifications have been gained, and how spiritual healing is thought to work. Healers will always ask new patients what medical advice and treatment they are receiving. Usually, people who seek the help of spiritual healers are very ill indeed: it is unusual to go for trivial complaints, although the illness may not always be physical. A healer cannot, of course, force a patient to go to a doctor, but will usually recommend this.

Spiritual healers will not, or should not, advise any particular course of medical treatment – that is considered outside their province. Instead, they will make you feel better by enabling you to relax and feel at peace so that self-healing can start to work. Very often, when hands are laid on you will feel a warmth, or even a cooling or tingling, as the energy starts to flow through the healer and into you.

Bona fide healers will not go into trance, ask you to take your clothes off, or indulge in any questionable practices which might make you frightened. If, as a woman patient, you are nervous of being alone with a male spiritual healer, you can always request a third party to be present during the session. Nor should healers offer any kind of clairvoyance during a session. The only thing they are permitted to do, if adhering to the spiritual healers' code of conduct, is to allow the healing energy to flow while they themselves are in a conscious frame of mind. Some healers may ask you to have an open mind on the subject of karma and reincarnation. It is not necessary for you to take on board the idea of reincarnation, but most present-day spiritual healers have come to feel that this is the only explanation for much of the illness and distress in the world.

But spiritual healers who are members of the NSFH will not take you back into past lives, hypnotize you or ask you to do anything that seems weird. In fact, most spiritual healers are very ordinary, down-to-earth people. But they all accept that basically we are spiritual, rather than merely physical beings. That is their principal difference from ordinary doctors and even alternative practitioners. Spiritual healers are above all working on the level of the spirit, rather than that of the body. If you don't like the idea of a soul, or spirit, or feel antagonism towards these terms, then just think of consciousness, attitude and approach instead. It is your attitude to life, relationships, other people, illness and so on which determines how well or ill you will be. Your mind creates the reality that becomes your body. Those who completely dismiss the idea of the soul, or who categorically deny that humans have such things, would very probably not benefit from spiritual healing. On the other hand, some highly sceptical people have gone to a spiritual healer simply because their condition has been so desperate that they were eventually willing to consider anything – and have found that their long-held beliefs (or unbeliefs) underwent a dramatic change. But nobody who is persistently hostile to the idea of spiritual healing should consider going to a healer.

Very often, though, great hostility or anger mask fear. It is frequently the case that those who maintain that their illness is purely physical – that there is no such thing as a human spirit, that we are only a collection of chemicals and nothing more – are terrified of facing themselves, of facing up to their health problem. A good spiritual healer will help patients to let go of fear and to gain the confidence to allow healing energy in.

Most spiritual healers work simply by laying on their hands: they will not attempt any vigorous massage or manipulation, although they may use gentle massage when laying on their hands. They will not use homeopathy, acupuncture, herbs or other potions. Not all healers actually make contact with the patient's body: some work with their hands a few inches away from the body. It is common practice for the healer to stand behind the seated patient, and lay lands on their shoulders or head.

Harry Kelly from East Molesey in Surrey who, like Edna Thorogood went to Jean Dreghorn's centre for help with his severe arthritis, was immediately aware of the effect of physical contact.

One of the healers, Barbara, said: 'Do you mind if I touch you?' and I said 'No.' She touched my head and then put her hands very gently on my knee. There was no pressure at all, and yet her hands seemed to burn right through me. The knee she was touching felt hot while the other was icy cold. Instantly, I felt a definite lessening of the pain, and my whole body seemed to relax.

After six weeks of treatment, Harry could walk easily.

So what will the healer be doing when he or she 'heals'? Although spiritual healing may sound airy-fairy, it is actually very specific, and simple to describe – although not necessarily so easy to achieve. As mentioned earlier, a spiritual healer is simply somebody who, for whatever reason, has the ability to channel energy from some outside source into you. But as the channel must be receptive to the energy, so the healer must be calm, confident and in a state of relaxation. Before you come for your healing session, the healer will have prepared for you – or should have done. The healer will have consciously changed his or her brainwaves into the alpha mode in order to channel the healing energy. Beware of any 'healer' who seems tense, under stress or anxious: if this is the case, it will be impossible to perform effective healing.

During a session, the healer will consciously focus thoughts on peace, love and light. He or she will visualize a flow of loving, peaceful energy coming into the body and into the healer's 'higher self'. The healer's mind will also be attuned to beautiful colours and will imagine new energy and a new level of health being created. Then, the healer will visualize this wonderful energy being released into you, the patient, and will see you in perfect health, being happy, healthy and filled with divine energy. That's really all there is to spiritual healing.

Some healers may suggest dietary changes, or recommend that you give up smoking or cut down on drinking, for example, but most see this kind of advice as outside their province. And no reputable healer will pretend to have medical qualifications, if they have not, or attempt to give this impression. For an effective healer, there is no need. The healer has a special gift of being able to channel extra energy: no other qualification is needed.

The availability of spiritual healing

Most healers work mainly from their own homes, or at their healing sanctuaries if they have them; they will also visit the housebound, or work in an NFSH healing centre or a group. Some people prefer group to individual healing, and this can be arranged; it is sometimes thought that healing energy is more concentrated when in a group.

The NFSH are now in the process of setting up a number of

healing centres up and down Britain so that they can operate in a similar way to the Red Cross or St John's Ambulance Brigade and be part of the local community services. There is not much likelihood in the near future of spiritual healing becoming available as a standard therapy on the NHS, although spiritual healers do work in hospitals, and some say they perform their best work in these places. Any seriously ill hospital patients can request to see a spiritual healer, and some hospitals have special days when healers come round the wards. But even in hospital, no healer will approach you without your permission.

Seeking out other forms of healing

If you wish to venture into the more esoteric realms of healing, to see a spiritualist healer or a past-life therapist, then there are still safeguards. All reputable spiritualist healers are members of the Spiritualist Association of Great Britain. People are not admitted as members until they have given some objective evidence that they possess mediumistic powers. Spiritualist healers work slightly differently from spiritual healers in that they believe they receive assistance from discarnate entities. Some may have spirit guides, or claim to channel a specific, usually long-dead person. Spiritualist healers may well go into a trance when they perform healing.

Those who are interested in contacting a Christian healer can contact the Churches' Council of Health and Healing. The Christian Church has become very much more open to the idea of healing now, and an increasing number of its ministers are practising laying on of hands. This type of Christian healing, as opposed to Christian Science healing, may not be so effective as that coming from actual spiritual healers. Some psychic people have told me that they have often seen auras around spiritual healers, but have never once seen an aura around an Anglican clergyman. Christian ministers who lay on hands do not always possess the special power that some spiritual healers undeniably have; they may be just doing their best, offering prayer and love, rather than being able to channel actual healing energy.

With past-life therapists, aura healers, colour healers and the like we are venturing into less charted territory. Mostly, people who specialize in very esoteric forms of healing do not exist in large enough numbers to be members of a professional organization; in any case, not all such people want to belong to specific groups. It doesn't mean that they are not trustworthy, but you may have to think hard about whether you want to put yourself in their hands. On the whole, most people who set up as healers of any kind – unless they are purveying unproven quack remedies at huge sums – do have a genuine wish to help. It is very unlikely that any harm will be done, and if you don't like the healer you don't need to go again. Whatever you do, never do anything like paying for six sessions in advance; always give the healer a trial first, and book up more sessions only if you feel you have benefitted.

Shirley Brooker, herself now a successful healer, had her first contact with spiritual healing when she went to a demonstration of trance healing after an osteopath had been unable to put right an agonising back strain caused by heavy lifting.

> *The demonstrator called me over, and started to run her hands gently down my back. She was hardly touching me, but suddenly there was a loud crack that everybody in the room could hear. From that time I was completely better, and never had another twinge. The cure was so quick and so remarkable that I decided to investigate the healing phenomenon properly, and joined the National Federation of Spiritual Healers. They don't give, or encourage, trance healing, and I don't do this form of healing either, but it certainly worked for me.*

As we saw in Chapter 3, healers really do seem to have something – although what that something is, nobody yet knows. It may just be that healers are people who are able to go easily into the alpha mode of consciousness, and that this ability to be calm and relaxed affects their patients. We are all very affected by atmosphere and vibrations, and it may be that the healing energy is nothing more than this. Certainly all the Mind Mirror experiments with known healers and psychics have shown up this alpha ability to a remarkable degree.

Alternatively, healers may be special recipients of some kind of extra-terrestrial healing energy, the source and content of which is as yet unknown. We cannot say for sure whether mediums and psychics are in contact with discarnate entities or spirit guides, or whether they are merely contacting their 'higher selves' – the self that lies beyond mundane needs and desires, the part of the self that can send out unconditional love.

But with all healers, whether they are spiritual, spiritualist, hypnotists or past-life therapists, the proof of the pudding must be in the eating. Ultimately, if we are very ill, we may not be all that concerned with how healing works; all we want to know is whether it does work. Those who are contemplating going to see a healer, but can't quite make up their mind, can always ask if it would be possible to contact some satisfied customers. No reputable healer would refuse to do this, as most present-day healers proceed by word-of-mouth recommendation.

Nineteen-year-old Arman Chaula developed severe rheumatoid arthritis at the age of fifteen. This meant that his life became severely restricted and his parents had to do everything for him, including getting him in and out of the bath and helping him to dress.

But because of spiritual healing, Arman has been able to take both O and A levels and go to college, where he is reading for a degree in economics. Arman has had to take a year off because of a severe flare-up but says that, thanks to spiritual healing, it is now gradually coming under control. He describes how he first got involved with healing:

All my muscles were wasting away, and I was losing weight rapidly, instead of gaining it, as I should have been as a fifteen-year-old. My parents were in despair – in spite of my being under the care of doctors at Northwick Park Hospital, which is one of the best-known centres for this disease, I was just getting worse.

Then a friend of my Dad's gave him a pamphlet about spiritual healing, and we decided we had nothing to lose. We contacted the healer – Shirley Brooker – and she came over to see me, as I couldn't get to see her. It made a definite difference straightaway.

It's well known that rheumatoid arthritis gets worse with stress, and Shirley concentrated on helping me to relax. I also feel tremendous heat in my joints when I have healing. Once my temperature went up to 102 degrees, just because of the healing.

The amazing thing is that Shirley can pick up the points where the aches and pains are worst, without me telling her. Although spiritual healing hasn't cured me, it has enabled me to live a normal life as a teenager, to play sport and drive a car. Also, I haven't got any physical deformities and I am absolutely certain that this is completely due to the healing. I look just like any other teenager, and nobody would know I have a chronic illness from looking at me.

I am on a lot of medication, but the drugs are toxic and can have bad side-effects, so they have to be carefully monitored. There is no doubt that healing lessens the pain considerably. I am now having healing once a fortnight, and always feel better.

It's hard to explain, but spiritual healing gives you a much more positive feeling about yourself. I would recommend it to anybody with a chronic condition.

Who can be a healer?

The short answer to this is: anybody. But as healing is an extremely responsible job, anybody who considers becoming a healer should look carefully into their own motivations. If there is a desire to become rich and famous through healing, or to have hundreds of people depending on and loving you, then it is probably better to think about another profession.

More usually, people become healers when there is already some indication that they possess healing powers. This happened with Major Bruce McManaway, when he laid hands on soldiers who had no access to medical treatment. He felt that something strange was happening, and often the men got better. Maurice Tester had no thoughts of becoming a healer until he went to Ted Fricker for treatment and was told the startling news: 'You're a healer, too.' George Chapman was apparently contacted by Dr William Lang when he was experimenting with clairvoyance during the long hours of waiting to be called out to fight a fire.

Allegra Taylor, author of *I Fly Out with Bright Feathers* (Subtitled *The Quest of a Novice Healer*), says that the idea that she might have healing powers came to her on the day her mother died, and she thought back to her mother's loving, gentle touch decades previously. Allegra says that in wanting to become a healer she was motivated by 'a tentative altruistic notion to want to help and heal others, to be able to offer something more useful than just a sympathetic ear to friends in time of sorrow or pain. Something practical.'

She had previously had some intimation that she might possess healing powers. In her book she writes about how she was stroking the hair of her sick youngest son one night and had

155

an impulse to raise her hand above his head. Almost at once, she writes, her whole arm began to tingle and her son's body – which had been racked with pain – became calm and peaceful. 'I knew then,' she wrote, 'with absolute certainty, that something stronger than me, something collective, was there when I needed to draw on it. It occurred to me that perhaps a healer can operate from an *intention* which utilizes the natural harmonious energy of the universe. Could I learn to harness this energy? Could I use it to be a better mother, a better friend?'

The possibility that she herself might be a healer sent Allegra, music teacher and journalist, right across the world, seeking out healers wherever she went, interviewing them, being with them and hoping to learn some secrets which might impart to her what healing was all about. She ends her book – and the quest – by saying that healing is one of humanity's greatest gifts. 'To me', she says, 'the continuous thread that wove together all the good healers I met was their capacity for unconditional love. I think therein lies the magic.'

Most healers would say that the only thing that motivates them is a love of their fellow humans. Unless you have this capacity for love, they say, you will be unable to heal. But, of course, 'love' is a very vague word. In this context it has nothing to do with being in love, with sexual passion, with a feeling of pity or attachment. The only possible love that can emanate from a healer is that which desires to see everybody in perfect health, fulfilling their potential, not hemmed in and hampered by stress, anxiety, addictions or negative emotions. Healers do not need to get anything back from their patients: they are on the receiving end of abundant energy, which they are passing on. In a sense, they are like a television or radio set, picking up waves of energy which they then transmit. Healers do not need anything from you, any more than a television set needs input from you – it works just the same whether you like it or not. People who want to get something back from their patients should never consider becoming healers – it's only when there is a feeling that you have energy and love to spare that this profession should be considered.

Potential healers should also bear in mind that the energy they may be able to tap is neutral, and can be used for good or evil. There is no doubt that extra energy can be generated by evil practices as well as good ones. Genuine healers have to wish everybody well, and not have likes and dislikes.

Those who feel they may have a gift for healing, and genuinely want to use this gift, can contact the NFSH who, as mentioned earlier, run courses for probationer healers. For although healing is primarily a gift, it can be improved with training and help from experts. The NFSH guidelines make it clear that it may not all be sweetness and light becoming a healer: you will have your failures and, more to the point, family and friends may be embarrassed by you and may not want to know you.

Healers, like practitioners of any other art, become more proficient by constant practice. Probationers are asked to develop their spirituality by reading and meditation. They should also work for a time with an accredited healer to gain experience and confidence. The 'bedside manner' is important, and is seen as part of the healing process.

Novice healers should not, say the guidelines, expect patients to beat a path to their door. But practice can always be gained with family and friends – ironically, nobody will object to you trying to 'heal' them if they have a splitting headache, an injury or feel depressed. There's more to being a healer, though, than having a few miracle successes. The most important attributes of a successful healer are self-awareness and spiritual growth.

Healers should always be non-judgemental in their approach, even when they have patients who have led very vicious, unhealthy or even criminal lives. No healing will ever take place unless there is a genuine feeling of love towards all patients, whatever their condition. Some people feel very uneasy around the ill and the afflicted; again, they are probably not healers by nature.

Healers should also themselves develop healthy habits of eating and living, otherwise the healing channel will not be clear and open. A sense of humour is a great asset – although, like healing itself, it is usually a gift rather than something which is learnt. Healers who can see the funny side of things are always in demand – nobody wants to be made to feel more miserable than before.

Most people, including healers, have to exercise constant vigilance over themselves in order to remain calm. But, says the

NFSH, people should never imagine they cannot be calm and happy, whatever external situations may be like. It is always possible to remain peaceful – there is never any absolute need to become stressed and anxious.

Healers, they say, should make efforts to simplify rather than complicate their lives, and should make sure they get rid of all unnecessary encumbrances. 'Always remember that to simplify your desires means a saving of energy', says a reminder on one of their sets of course notes. Healers have to make efforts to conserve their own strength and energy, rather than draining it by bad diets, smoking, drinking or having a wild sex life. Even leisure time should be used constructively – no time should ever be wasted or frittered away. Every useless activity, every waste thought, blocks and confuses the energy channels.

Healers have to live in the present, not hark back to the past, have regrets about what might have been, or worry about what might happen in the future. Dwelling unduly on either the past or the future fills the mind with unnecessary worries and negativities. There should be no blame attached to anybody, including oneself. Healers will not always succeed, and they will undoubtedly make mistakes, but they should never lose faith in themselves, or imagine they are no good. As soon as belief in oneself is shaken, the healing ability recedes.

Although healing ability is in many ways a gift, serenity, poise, self-esteem and self-confidence are attributes that can be learnt. The more you are able to inculcate them in your everyday life, says the NFSH, the more they will become part of you. And it is your serenity and poise which will attract other people to you.

It is not an easy task to be a healer. Although it may sound very attractive and rewarding, healing takes up the whole of a person's time and thought. Healers have to remember, says the NFSH, that healing is not just laying on of hands in a sanctuary, or sending out absent healing from time to time. Unlike most professions, this one cannot be switched off, and healing must be seen as a permanent way of life. The healing will always be what comes first in a healer's life, before personal relationships and personal satisfactions. That is why people are often middle-aged before they become professional healers: they may have to wait until everything else – home, family, love, sex – has been accomplished and no longer plays an important part. The greatest danger for any successful healer is ego. This is why they must be careful not to accept adulation from their grateful patients, and to keep reminding themselves that the healing energy comes through them, not from them, and that they are privileged to be such a channel.

❧ *Glossary*

Aura
Spiritual healers and clairvoyants maintain that each individual possesses an aura, a kind of coloured glow surrounding the body. This aura, invisible to most people and impossible to detect by normal scientific means, changes colour according to the individual's state of health, say healers. Thus a grey, dingy aura would indicate ill health, while a brightly-coloured sparkling aura means the person is extremely healthy. 'Aura diagnosis' is often employed by spiritual healers.

Automatic art
This is a form of art produced in a trance state. Usually, the 'artist' does not know the drawings or paintings have been produced and is unable to execute them during normal conscious states. Most automatic art is of very poor technical quality, although a few healers and psychics have been able to produce drawings of a higher standard than they can achieve ordinarily.

Automatic writing
Similar to automatic art, in that it is produced in a trance state, with the individual having no idea of what is being written. Some clairvoyants claim to be able to receive messages from 'the other side' which they then write down when in an unconscious state: sometimes they claim to be taken over by a discarnate entity whose hand is holding the pen. Most

automatic writing is very characteristic in appearance, being shaky and spidery and difficult to read.

Autonomic nervous system
This is used to refer to involuntary actions which we cannot prevent, such as breathing, blood pressure, digestion, the passage of hormones and so on. It is the body's self-working system and not normally under conscious control.

Biofeedback
A technique which enables people to gain control over normally non-controllable, or autonomic, functions of the body. There are several types of biofeedback device available which can monitor small changes in blood pressure and body temperatures. Through relaxation, yoga or other forms of training, people can learn to reduce their blood pressure, sweating, or other signs of anxiety or tension, and can direct heat into their hands and feet, for example.

Chakras
According to ancient yogic doctrines, the chakras are a series of energy centres throughout the body. They operate as conduits between the physical and the etheric bodies, allowing *prana*, or universal energy, to flow through the system. The word is Sanskrit for wheel, and chakras are considered to be dynamic powerhouses of energy. There are 13 chakras in all in the human body, and seven main ones. Each chakra has a different frequency, colour and sound. Illness occurs, according to the doctrine, when a chakra becomes blocked and energy cannot flow properly. Spiritual healers may concentrate on unblocking the chakras, although not all healers use this term.

Channelling
A term of American origin (where it is spelt *channeling*) used to denote the supposed ability of some people to act as a neutral conduit through which healing energy flows. Most spiritual healers would consider themselves channels; that is, the healing comes through them rather than from them. Channelling also refers to the clairvoyant ability to contact discarnate entities and dispense their words of wisdom to a wider audience.

Cosmic consciousness

Some healers and psychics maintain that the cosmos has a consciousness all of its own, and that this can be tapped for healing purposes. Recent scientific work on astrology has indicated that planetary configurations really do influence our lives and characters; so perhaps the day will come when it is proved that the cosmos has some influence as well. Most healers maintain that cosmic energy is beneficial, so long as we know how to use it.

Double-blind

A method of conducting clinical trials whereby the volunteers have no knowledge of what is being tested: in a typical double-blind trial, half the subjects will be given the active drug and the other half the placebo, but nobody apart from the researcher will know which group takes what. Double-blind is the generally accepted method of carrying out tests for new drugs and treatments.

EEG (electroencephalograph) machine

A machine which records the brain's electrical activity by means of electrodes placed on the patient's head. Medically, EEGs are used to record abnormal brain wave patterns to diagnose certain illnesses such as epilepsy, tumours and brain disorders.

Etheric body

In esoteric doctrines, each person has an invisible 'etheric body' surrounding the physical one, which it exactly mirrors. If the physical body has an illness, so will the etheric body. Many spiritual healers claim to be able to work on the etheric body, in the belief that the physical body will then be cured. Although psychics have often claimed to see the etheric body, its existence has never been scientifically shown in any way; it remains an aspect of belief.

Karma

A Sanskrit word meaning 'action'. In simple terms, it refers to the doctrine that as you sow, so shall you reap. A universal law of cause and effect, an individual's 'karma' is the sum of good and bad actions accumulated through many lifetimes: the doctrine is integral to the concept of reincarnation. In fact, reincarnation has little meaning or importance without karma being understood as well.

M.E. disease

The letters M.E. stand for myalgic encephalomyelitis, and refer to inflammation of the brain (encaphalo-), usually caused by viral infection. The term 'myalgic' refers to muscles, and 'myelitis' to the myelin sheath in the brain. The word is new and has been constructed by the medical profession to describe the symptoms of this disease.

New Age

According to astrologers, we are now entering the planetary 'New Age' of Aquarius, which will be characterized by peace, love and harmony. Generally, the term is used to describe anything alternative, non-hierarchical, co-operative, organic – working in harmony with nature and one's fellow humans instead of in competition with them.

Paranormal

A general term used to denote anything which appears to be beyond the normal, and used with reference to ghosts, elemental beings, metal bending, telepathy – in fact, anything which seems to defy rational or scientific explanation and yet which cannot be completely dismissed owing to the large body of 'anecdotal' evidence.

Placebo effect

Literally, from the Latin: 'I will please'. Used to denote the belief that a particular medication or treatment will do good, even though it may contain no pharmacologically active ingredient. In medicine, 'placebo' means a dummy, inert pill. Such is the power of suggestion that placebos often have almost as dramatic an effect as actual medication, and sometimes more so.

Psychosomatic

Diseases which have both a physical and emotional component: from the Greek 'psyche', meaning mind, and 'soma', to do with the body. It is increasingly accepted that most, if not all, diseases have a psychosomatic element, and that there is no such thing as a purely physical disease.

Regression
In psychoanalysis, a term donoting going back to childhood or birth with the aid of a therapist to uncover and bring to the surface repressed and consciously forgotten traumas. Some hypnotists are now also using past-life regression, to take patients back to a previous life, in the belief that not every present problem can be unravelled with reference only to the current incarnation.

Remission
Many modern chronic diseases are characterized by periods of extreme illness followed by times of relative or even absolute health, for no apparent reason; this phase is known as 'going into remission'. Many orthodox doctors believe that spiritual healing is no more than taking credit for spontaneous periods of remission.

Shaman
An anthropological term used to describe a doctor who also combines the functions of a priest. The shaman is supposedly able to communicate with the spirit world during trance states. He (most shamans in ancient times were male) may also have been able to divine the future and perform magic. Shamans are apparently able to affect subtle energy systems of which most people are unaware. Traditionally, shamans were highly respected by tribal societies.

Selected Bibliography

Baerlein, E. and Dower, A. L. G. *Healing with Radionics*, Thorsons, 1980

Bailey, Alice *Esoteric Healing*, Lucis Publishing Company, 1953

Bek, Lilla and Pullar, Philippa *The Seven Levels of Healing*, Rider, 1986

Blades, Rev Dudley *Spiritual Healing: The Power of the Gentle Touch*, Aquarian, 1979

Cade, Maxwell and Coxhead, Nona *The Awakened Mind*, Wildwood House, 1980

Chapman, George *Surgeon from Another World*, as told to Roy Stemman, Psychic Press, 1988

Cooke, Ivan *Healing By The Spirit*, White Eagle Publishing Trust, 1980

Edwards, Harry *The Power of Spiritual Healing*, The Harry Edwards Spiritual Healing Sanctuary Trust, 1963

Harvey, David *The Power to Heal: An Investigation of Healing and Healing Experiences*, Aquarian, 1983

Hay, Louise L. *Heal Your Body: The Mental Causes for Physical Illness and the Metaphysical Way to Overcome Them*, Heaven on Earth Books, 1984 and *You Can Heal Your Life*, Eden Grove Editions, 1988

Herzberg, Eileen *Spiritual Healing: A Patient's Guide*, Thorsons, 1988

Holmes, Ernest *The Science of Mind*, Dodd, Mead and Co, New York, 1959

Hutton, J. Bernard *Healing Hands*, W. H. Allen, 1982

Hutton, J. Bernard *The Healing Power*, Leslie Frewin, 1970

Levine, Stephen *Healing into Life and Death*, Gateway Books, 1987

Manning, Matthew *Matthew Manning's Guide to Self-Healing*, Thorsons, 1989

McManaway, Bruce with Johanna Turcan *Spiritual Healing*, Thorsons, 1983

Meel, George, ed. *Healers and the Healing Process*, Quest Books, 1977

Peel, Robert *Spiritual Healing in a Scientific Age*, Harper and Row, 1988

Pitts, John *Divine Healing: Fact or Fiction*, Arthur James Ltd, 1962

Playfair, Guy Lyon *If This Be Magic*, Cape, 1985

Pleshette, Janet *Cures that Work*, Century Arrow, 1986

Pullar, Philippa *Spiritual and Lay Healing*, Penguin, 1988

Randi, James *The Faith Healers*, Prometheus Books, 1987

Sharma, I. C. *Cayce, Karma and Reincarnation*, Quest Books, 1975

Shine, Betty *Mind to Mind*, Bantam, 1989

Taylor, Allegra *I Fly Out with Bright Feathers: The Quest of a Novice Healer*, Fontana, 1987

Tester, M. H. *The Healing Touch*, Psychic Press, 1970

Useful Addresses

The National Federation of
   Spiritual Healers,
Old Manor Farm Studio,
Church Street,
Sunbury on Thames,
Middlesex TW16 6RG.
Tel: 0932 783164/5

Runs courses on spiritual healing
and offers a code of conduct to
members and people wishing to
practise this form of healing. Also
has lists of accredited spiritual
healers.

The Confederation of Healing
   Organisations,
113 Hampstead Way,
London NW11 7JN.

Has lists of members and affiliates
who operate within the ethical code
of the CHO.

The Divine Healing Mission,
The Old Rectory,
Crowhurst, Sussex TN33 9AD.
Tel: 042483 204

Christian laying on of hands
healing. Residential.

Burrswood,
Groombridge,
Tunbridge Wells,
Kent TN3 9PY.

Christian healing services.

Soul·Directed Astrology,
5a Cedar Road,
Sutton, Surrey SM2 5DA.
Tel: 081-643 4898

Spiritual healing using astrology.

St Marylebone Pastoral Centre,
17 Marylebone Road,
London NW1 5LT.
Tel: 071-935 6374

Holds Christian healing services
and counselling sessions. Also the
HQ of the Churches' Council for
Health and Healing.

Science of Mind,
c/o The Hale Clinic,
7 Park Crescent,
London W1N 3HE.
Tel: 071-637 3377

'Scientific Prayer' available for
healing purposes.

Matthew Manning Centre,
39 Abbeygate Street,
Bury St Edmunds,
Suffolk IP33 1LW.
Tel: 0284 752364

Specialises in healing of the
seriously ill, including cancer
patients.

College of Healing,
Runnings Park,
Croft Bank,
West Malvern,
Worcs WR14 4BP.
Tel: 06845 65253

Affiliated to the Wrekin Trust.
Holds regular courses on aspects of
healing.

The Spiritualist Association of
   Great Britain,
33 Belgrave Square,
London SW1X 8QC.
Tel: 071-235 3351

Holds regular healing sessions at this and other venues.

Maitreya School of Healing,
37 Third Avenue,
Bexhill on Sea,
Sussex TN40 2PA.
Tel: 0424 211450

Guild of Spiritualist Healers,
36 Newmarket,
Otley,
West Yorks LS21 3AE.
Tel: 0535 681974

White Eagle Lodge,
New Lands,
Brewells Lane,
Rake,
Liss,
Hampshire GU33 7HY.
Tel: 0733 893300

George Chapman,
Chapman's House,
Pant Glas,
Tre'r-ddol,
Machynlleth,
Mid Wales.

The Harry Edwards Spiritual
Healing Sanctuary Trust,
Burrow's Lea,
Shere,
Guildford, Surrey GU5 9QG.

Ursula Fleming Tapes,
Flat 1,
25 Upper Park Road,
London NW3 2UN.

In Australia:

The Australian Spiritual Healers'
Association,
PO Box 4073,
8 Mile Plains,
Queensland 4113,
Australia.

In New Zealand:

New Zealand Federation of
Spiritual Healers, Inc.
PO Box 9502,
Newmarket,
Auckland,
New Zealand.

Index